Letts

GCSE

VISUAL REVISION GUIDE

SUCCESS

CHEMISTRY

Author

Emma Poole

CONTENTS

EARTH MATERIALS

Revised

METALS

Revised

STRUCTURE AND BONDING

CHEMICAL CHANGE

LIMESTONE

Limestone is a <u>sedimentary</u> rock. It is mainly <u>calcium carbonate</u>. It can be <u>quarried</u> and cut into blocks which can be used for <u>building</u>.

If the limestone is powdered it can be used to <u>neutralise</u> the <u>acidity in lakes caused by acid rain</u> and to <u>neutralise acidic soils</u>.

HEATING LIMESTONE

- When <u>limestone</u> (<u>calcium carbonate</u>) is <u>heated it breaks down</u> to form <u>quicklime</u> (<u>calcium oxide</u>) and <u>carbon dioxide</u> (CO_2).

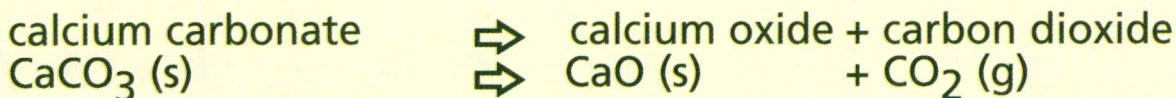

calcium carbonate $\Rightarrow$ calcium oxide + carbon dioxide
$CaCO_3$ (s) $\Rightarrow$ CaO (s) + CO_2 (g)

This is an example of a thermal decomposition reaction.

- The <u>quicklime</u> (<u>calcium oxide</u>) reacts with water to form <u>slaked lime</u> (calcium hydroxide). A solution of slaked lime is known as <u>limewater</u>.

calcium oxide + water $\Rightarrow$ calcium hydroxide
CaO (S) + H_2O (l) $\Rightarrow$ $Ca(OH)_2$ (s)

- Because they are both bases, slaked lime can be used in the same way as powdered limestone in lakes and on soils, but it works much more quickly.

Examiner's Top Tip
Learn the equation involved when limestone is heated.

REACTION SUMMARY

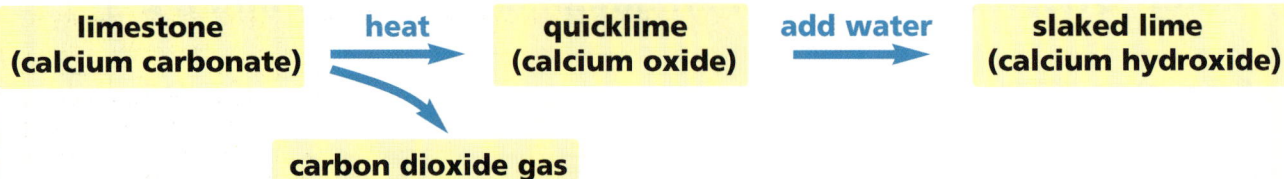

limestone (calcium carbonate) —heat→ quicklime (calcium oxide) —add water→ slaked lime (calcium hydroxide)

carbon dioxide gas

OTHER USES OF LIMESTONE

GLASS

Glass can be made by <u>heating</u> up a mixture of <u>limestone</u> (calcium carbonate), <u>sand</u> (silicon dioxide) and <u>soda</u> (sodium carbonate) until the mixture melts.

CEMENT

Cement is produced by <u>roasting</u> <u>powdered</u> <u>clay</u> with powdered <u>limestone</u> in a rotating kiln.

If the <u>cement</u> is mixed with <u>water</u>, <u>sand</u> <u>and</u> <u>rock</u> <u>chippings</u> a slow chemical reaction produces the <u>rock-like</u> <u>concrete</u>.

Concrete is hard and cheap and is widely used in building.

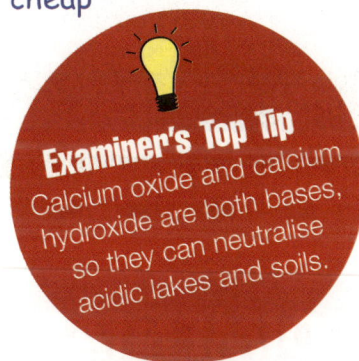

Examiner's Top Tip
Calcium oxide and calcium hydroxide are both bases, so they can neutralise acidic lakes and soils.

QUICK TEST

1. What is the main chemical in limestone?
2. What type of rock is limestone?
3. What is powdered limestone used for?
4. What is formed when limestone is heated?
5. What is the equation for this reaction?
6. What type of reaction is this?
7. What is formed when quicklime (calcium oxide) is reacted with water?
8. What is the equation for this reaction?
9. How is glass made?
10. How is cement made, and what can it be made into?

10. Roasting powdered clay + limestone; can be made into concrete
9. Heating limestone, sand and soda
8. $CaO(s) + H_2O(l) \longrightarrow Ca(OH)_2(s)$
7. Slaked lime/calcium hydroxide
6. Thermal decomposition
5. $CaCO_3(s) \longrightarrow CaO(s) + CO_2(g)$
4. Quicklime/calcium oxide and carbon dioxide
3. Neutralise acidity in soils/lakes
2. Sedimentary
1. Calcium carbonate

IGNEOUS ROCKS

- All **igneous rocks** are formed from **molten rock** which has **cooled** and **solidified**. Molten rock below the surface of the Earth is called magma, above the Earth's surface it is called lava.

- **Igneous rocks** are very hard and have **crystals**.

- **Extrusive igneous rocks** have **small crystals** because they have formed very quickly above ground. Basalt is an example of an extrusive igneous rock.

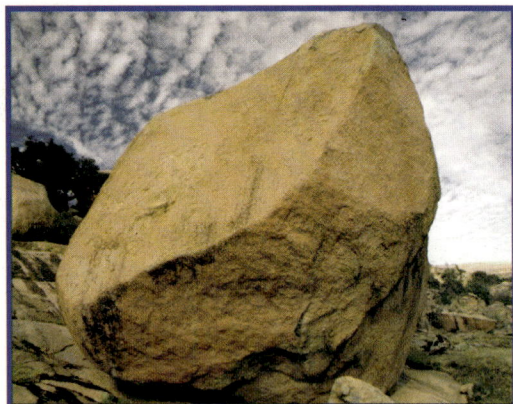

granite has large crystals

- **Intrusive igneous rocks** have **large crystals** because they solidified slowly below the ground. Granite is an example of an intrusive igneous rock.

SEDIMENTARY ROCKS

- *Sedimentary rocks* tend to be *crumbly* and sometimes contain *fossils*. Sandstone and limestone are examples of sedimentary rocks.

sandstone

limestone

- *Sedimentary rocks* form from *layers of sediment* found in seas or lakes. Over millions of years these layers are buried by further sediment. The weight of these layers *squeezes out the water* and the *particles become cemented together*.

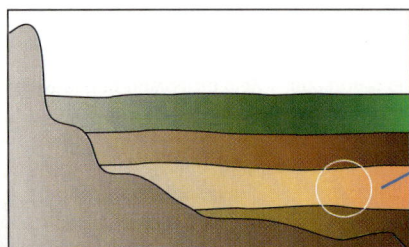

layers of sediment build up

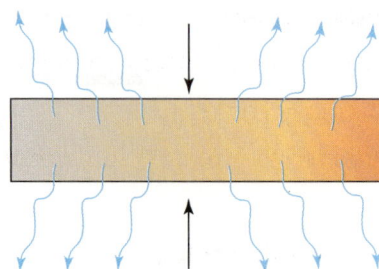

water is squeezed out

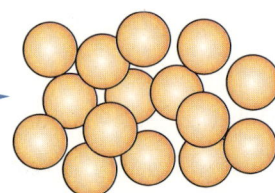

the particles of rock become cemented together

METAMORPHIC ROCKS

schist (schist and gneiss are examples of metamorphic rocks)

Metamorphic rocks are usually hard and may contain banded crystals. Metamorphic rocks are formed by high temperature and pressure on existing rocks. Metamorphic rocks can be formed when rock is stressed as mountains are formed or when hot magma comes into contact with rock causing alteration of the existing rocks.

ROCKS CAN BE CLASSIFIED INTO 3 GROUPS:
IGNEOUS, SEDIMENTARY AND METAMORPHIC ROCKS

QUICK TEST

1. Which type of rock is formed when molten rock cools and solidifies?

2. Which type of rock is the hardest?

3. Which sort of igneous rock has small crystals and was formed quickly?

4. Which sort of igneous rock has large crystals and was formed slowly?

5. Give two examples of igneous rocks.

6. Which type of rock may contain fossils?

7. Over what sort of time period do sedimentary rocks form?

8. Give two examples of sedimentary rocks.

9. What two factors can cause existing rock to be changed into metamorphic rock?

10. Give two examples of metamorphic rocks.

1. Igneous
2. Igneous
3. Extrusive e.g. basalt
4. Intrusive e.g. granite
5. Basalt and granite
6. Sedimentary
7. Millions of years
8. Sandstone, limestone
9. Heat, pressure
10. Schist, gneiss

CLUES IN ROCKS

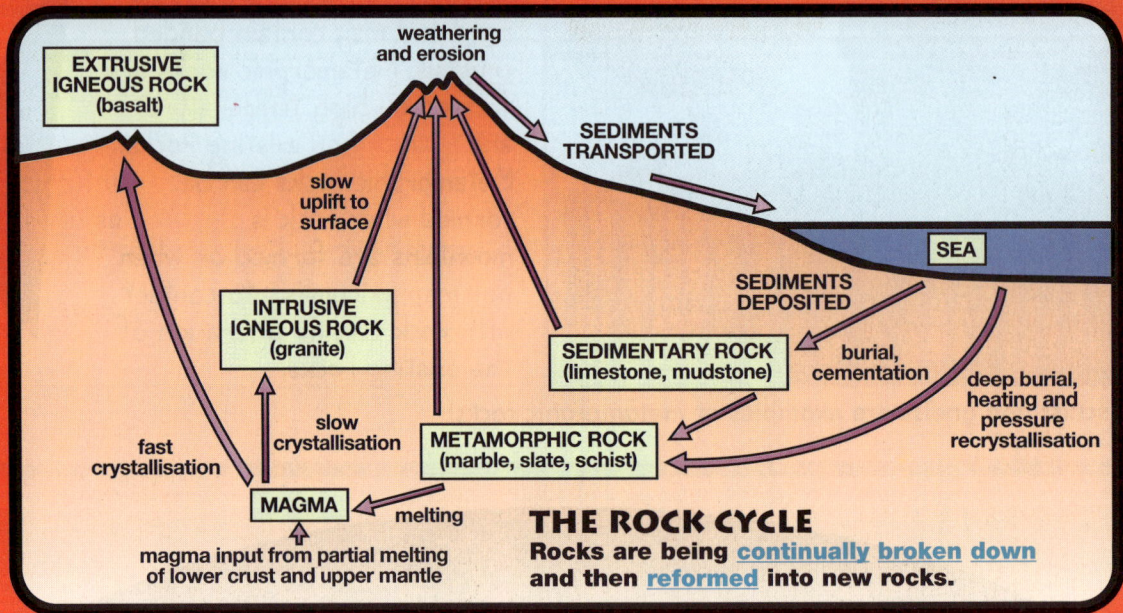

EXTRUSIVE IGNEOUS ROCK (basalt)

weathering and erosion

SEDIMENTS TRANSPORTED

slow uplift to surface

SEA

SEDIMENTS DEPOSITED

INTRUSIVE IGNEOUS ROCK (granite)

SEDIMENTARY ROCK (limestone, mudstone)

burial, cementation

deep burial, heating and pressure recrystallisation

slow crystallisation

METAMORPHIC ROCK (marble, slate, schist)

fast crystallisation

MAGMA   melting

magma input from partial melting of lower crust and upper mantle

THE ROCK CYCLE
Rocks are being continually broken down and then reformed into new rocks.

SEDIMENTARY ROCKS

- Sedimentary rocks are formed when particles are deposited by water, wind or ice.
- The rocks build up in layers.
- The youngest rocks are usually found on top of older rocks.

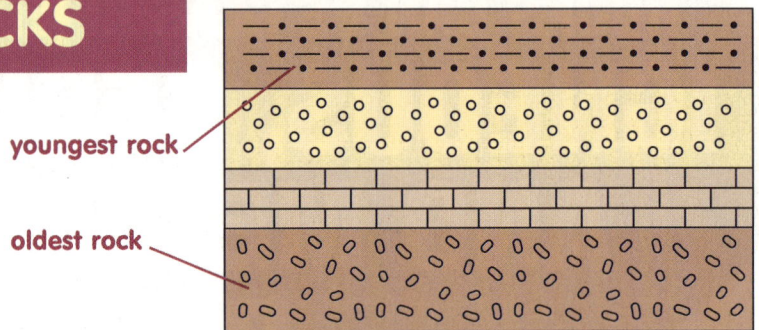

youngest rock

oldest rock

IGNEOUS ROCKS

Igneous rocks can also give useful information about the geological history of an area. Igneous rocks sometimes intrude into existing sedimentary rocks.

This can be used to date the age of the rocks. The igneous rock must be younger than the sedimentary rock that it cuts across.

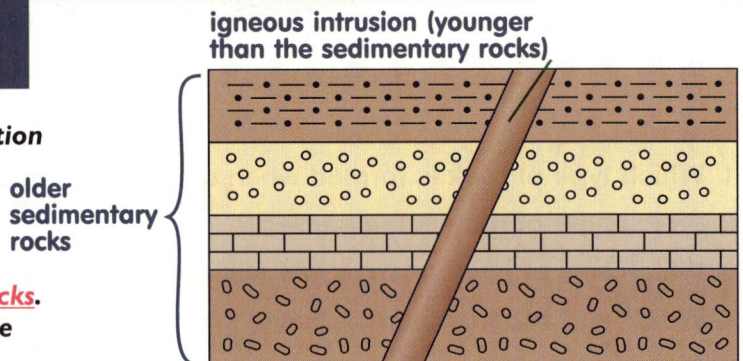

igneous intrusion (younger than the sedimentary rocks)

older sedimentary rocks

RIPPLE MARKS

- **Ripple marks** (parallel ridges) are sometimes seen in sedimentary rocks. They are **formed by the movement** of currents and waves as the particles were **deposited in the sea**.

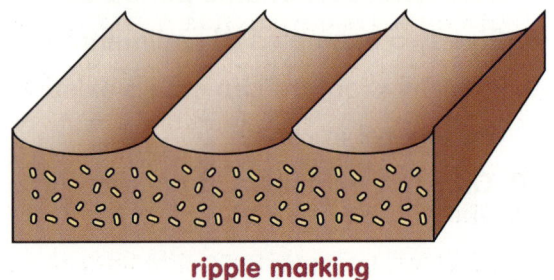

ripple marking

FOLDING

Rock layers may become bent due to the forces they are subjected to. This is a fold:

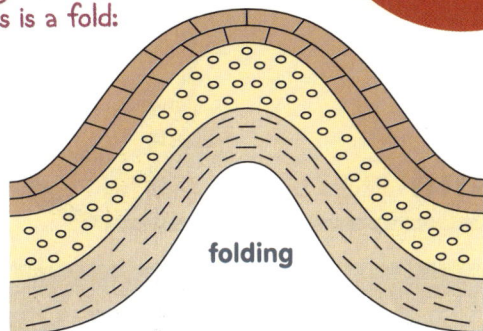

folding

Sometimes the forces on the existing rocks are so great that they can even be overturned.

Examiner's Top Tip
Now cover this page over and try to write down the ideas.

FAULTING

- Sedimentary rocks can be subjected to great forces as the plates move.
- The rock may be subjected to so much force that it snaps.

This is a fault:

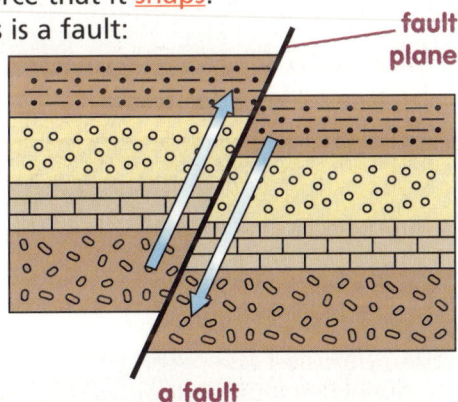

fault plane

a fault

DISCONTINUOUS DEPOSITION

Sedimentary rocks can give a lot of information about what was happening at the time the rock was formed.

A discontinuous deposition shows that there was a period of erosion followed by a later period where sediment was again deposited.

These discontinuities can occur over large areas and indicate that there was a relative movement of the land and the sea.

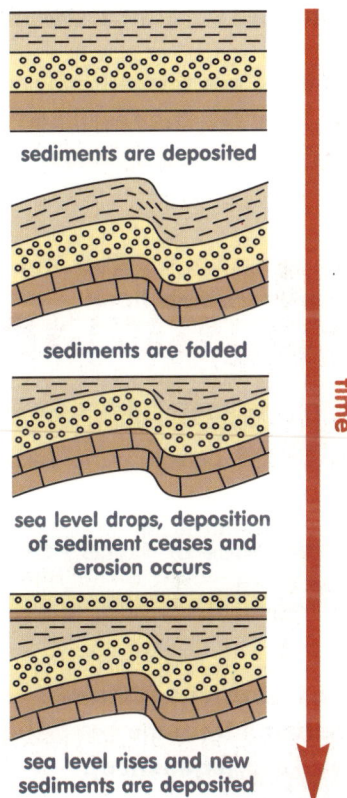

sediments are deposited

sediments are folded

time

sea level drops, deposition of sediment ceases and erosion occurs

sea level rises and new sediments are deposited

QUICK TEST

1. How are sedimentary rocks turned into metamorphic rocks?
2. If magma is crystallised quickly what type of rock is formed?
3. If magma is crystallised slowly what type of rock is formed?
4. Why are younger rocks normally found on top of older rocks?
5. What causes ripple marks on rocks?
6. An igneous intrusion is found to have cut across sedimentary rock, what can be deduced about the ages of the rocks?
7. Why are some rocks faulted or folded?
8. Sketch what happens when a sedimentary rock is faulted.
9. Sketch what happens when a sedimentary rock is folded.
10. Sketch the stages which lead to discontinuous deposition.

10. Refer to diagrams above
9. Refer to diagrams above
8. Refer to diagrams above
7. Forces as plates move
6. Igneous younger than sedimentary
5. Movement of currents/waves
4. Deposited later on top of existing rock
3. Intrusive igneous rocks
2. Extrusive igneous rocks
1. Heat + pressure

9

FOSSIL FUELS

OIL

Fossil fuels are <u>coal</u>, <u>oil</u> and <u>natural gas</u>.

FORMATION OF COAL, OIL AND NATURAL GAS

Fossil fuels are formed over <u>millions of years</u>. They are the fossilised remains of <u>dead plants and animals</u>.

<u>Plants and animals</u> died and fell to the sea or swamp floor.

The remains were quickly covered by <u>sediment</u>.

In the absence of <u>oxygen</u> the remains did not <u>decay</u>.

As the layers of sediment <u>increased</u> the remains became <u>heated and pressurised</u> (squashed).

After millions of years <u>coal</u>, <u>oil and natural gas</u> are formed.

Dead plants falling into swamps form <u>coal</u>, while tiny dead sea creatures and plants form <u>oil and natural gas</u>.

Burning fossil fuels is an exothermic process giving out a lot of heat.

Fossil fuels are <u>non-renewable</u>. They take millions of years to form, but they are being used up very quickly.

TIME

tree falling into swamp

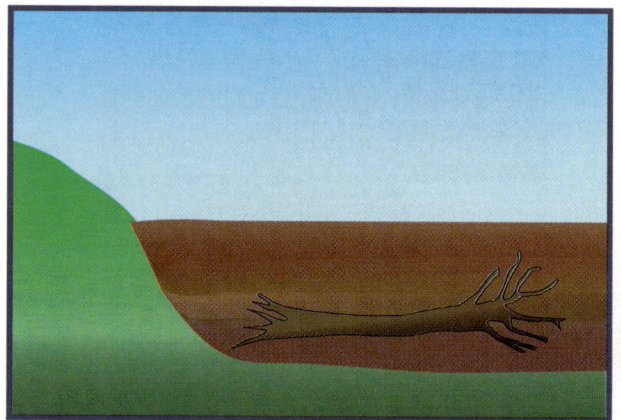

millions of years pass

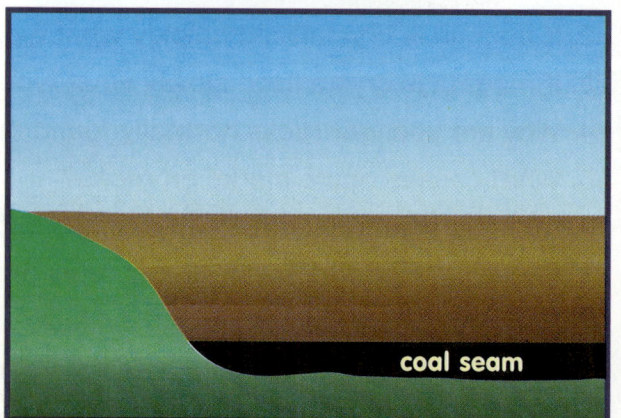

coal seam

coal is formed

FRACTIONAL DISTILLATION OF CRUDE OIL

Crude oil is a mixture of hydrocarbons.
Hydrocarbons are molecules that contain only hydrogen and carbon atoms.
Some of the hydrocarbons have very short chains of carbon atoms.
These hydrocarbons are runny, easy to ignite and have low boiling points.
Other hydrocarbons have much longer chains of carbon atoms. These hydrocarbons are more viscous (less runny), harder to ignite and have higher boiling points.
This means that long chain hydrocarbons are not useful as fuels.

Fractional distillation can be used to split mixtures of hydrocarbons (crude oil). In the fractionating column the bottom is kept very hot, while the top of the column is much cooler.
The smallest molecules (those with the lowest boiling points) boil off first and rise to the top of the column.
The other fractions are collected at different points down the column.

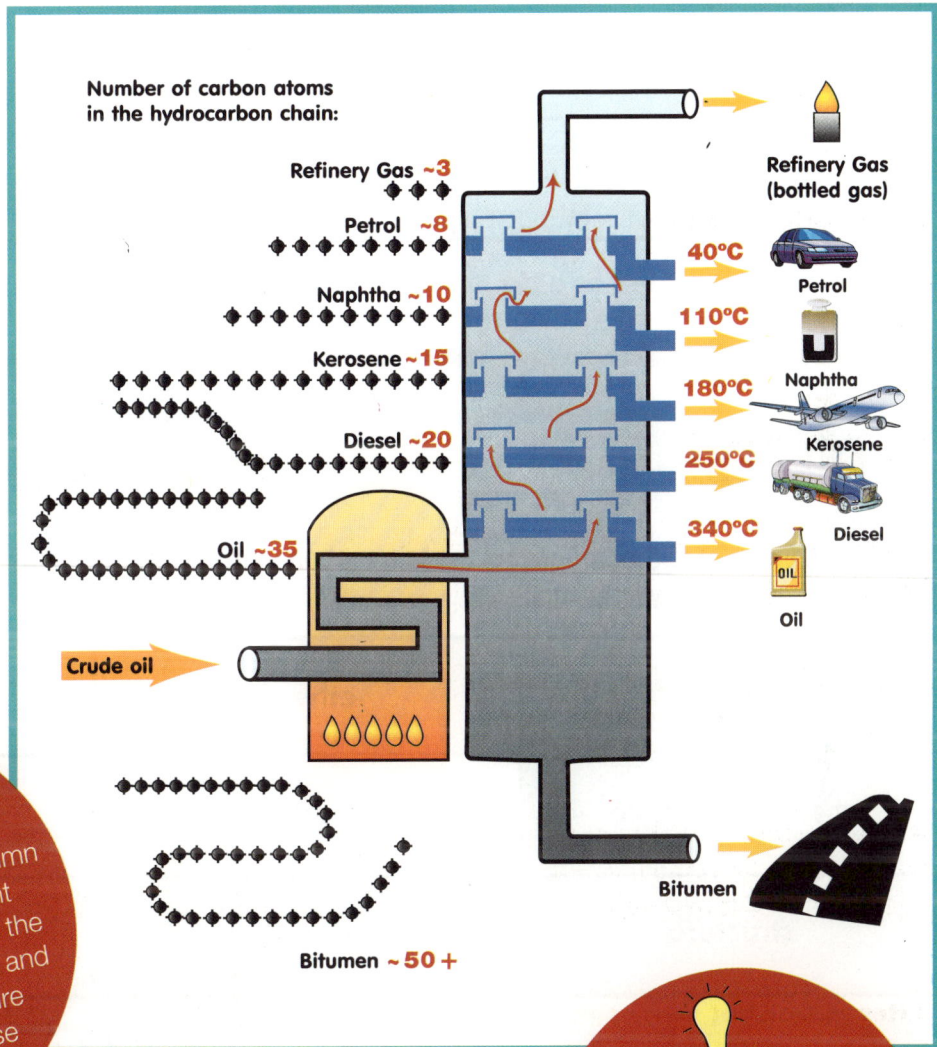

Number of carbon atoms in the hydrocarbon chain:

Refinery Gas ~3
Petrol ~8
Naphtha ~10
Kerosene ~15
Diesel ~20
Oil ~35

Crude oil

Bitumen ~ 50 +

Refinery Gas (bottled gas)

40°C Petrol
110°C Naphtha
180°C Kerosene
250°C Diesel
340°C Oil

Bitumen

Examiner's Top Tip
Look at the fractionating column diagram, learn the different number of carbon atoms in the hydrocarbons, their names and uses and the temperature at which they condense and can be collected.

Examiner's Top Tip
Remember plants and animals are only fossilised if no air reaches them; if oxygen does reach them the remains will decay.

QUICK TEST

1. Over what kind of time scale are fossil fuels formed?
2. Why are they named fossil fuels?
3. Why do some sediments not decay?
4. From what is coal formed?
5. From what are oil and natural gas formed?
6. What atoms do hydrocarbons contain?

1. Millions of years
2. Fossilised remains of plants/animals
3. No oxygen
4. Dead plants
5. Tiny sea creatures and plants
6. Carbon and hydrogen

ALKANES

All hydrocarbons have a spine of carbon atoms.
Molecules that belong to the alkane family contain no carbon–carbon double covalent bonds.
They are saturated hydrocarbons.

Name	methane	ethane	propane	butane
chemical formula	CH_4	C_2H_6	C_3H_8	C_4H_{10}
structure	$\begin{array}{c} H \\ | \\ H-C-H \\ | \\ H \end{array}$	$\begin{array}{c} H\ H \\ |\ \ | \\ H-C-C-H \\ |\ \ | \\ H\ H \end{array}$	$\begin{array}{c} H\ H\ H \\ |\ \ |\ \ | \\ H-C-C-C-H \\ |\ \ |\ \ | \\ H\ H\ H \end{array}$	$\begin{array}{c} H\ H\ H\ H \\ |\ \ |\ \ |\ \ | \\ H-C-C-C-C-H \\ |\ \ |\ \ |\ \ | \\ H\ H\ H\ H \end{array}$

Alkanes are unreactive and do not react with bromine water.

ALKENES

The alkene family of hydrocarbons do contain carbon–carbon double bonds.
They are unsaturated hydrocarbons.

name	ethene	propene
chemical formula	C_2H_4	C_3H_6
structure	$\begin{array}{c} H\ \ \ \ \ \ \ \ H \\ \backslash\ \ \ \ \ / \\ C = C \\ /\ \ \ \ \ \backslash \\ H\ \ \ \ \ \ \ \ H \end{array}$	$\begin{array}{c} H\ \ \ \ \ \ \ \ \ \ \ \ \ \ H \\ \backslash\ \ \ \ \ \ \ \ \ \ \ \ | \\ C = C - C - H \\ /\ \ \ \ \ \ |\ \ \ \ | \\ H\ \ \ \ \ H\ \ \ H \end{array}$

Alkenes are more reactive than alkanes because of their carbon–carbon double bonds.
This means that alkenes are useful for making new substances, including polymers.
Alkenes do react with bromine water, turning it from orange-brown to colourless.

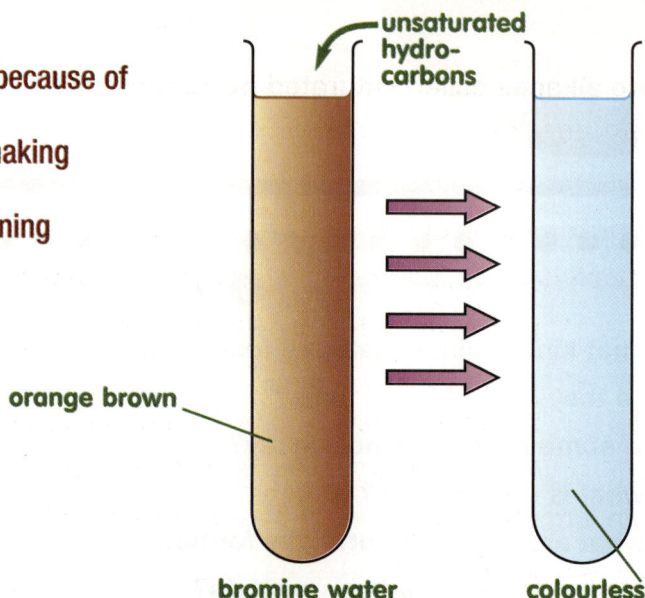

unsaturated hydro-carbons

orange brown

bromine water

colourless

CRACKING

The large hydrocarbons separated during the fractional distillation of crude oil are not very useful. Cracking can break down these large hydrocarbons into smaller, more useful molecules. There is more demand and therefore a higher price for the smaller hydrocarbons like petrol compared with larger molecules like lubricating oil.

CRACKING

Crude oil contains a mixture of hydrocarbons.

INDUSTRIAL CRACKING

The hydrocarbons are heated, so that they vaporise. They are then passed over a hot aluminium oxide catalyst.

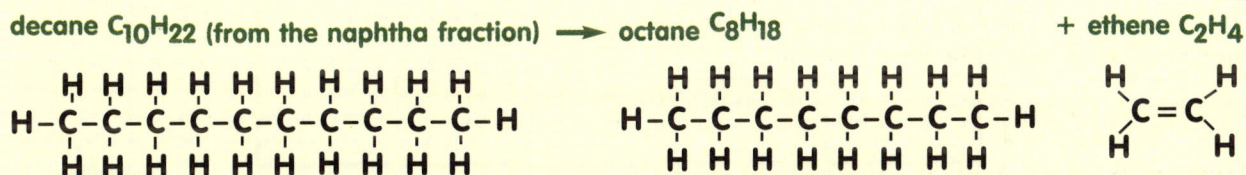

decane $C_{10}H_{22}$ (from the naphtha fraction) $\longrightarrow$ octane C_8H_{18} $+$ ethene C_2H_4

$$H-\overset{\displaystyle H}{\underset{\displaystyle H}{C}}-\overset{\displaystyle H}{\underset{\displaystyle H}{C}}-\overset{\displaystyle H}{\underset{\displaystyle H}{C}}-\overset{\displaystyle H}{\underset{\displaystyle H}{C}}-\overset{\displaystyle H}{\underset{\displaystyle H}{C}}-\overset{\displaystyle H}{\underset{\displaystyle H}{C}}-\overset{\displaystyle H}{\underset{\displaystyle H}{C}}-\overset{\displaystyle H}{\underset{\displaystyle H}{C}}-\overset{\displaystyle H}{\underset{\displaystyle H}{C}}-\overset{\displaystyle H}{\underset{\displaystyle H}{C}}-H$$

Octane is used in petrol and the ethene which is also produced is used to make plastics.

QUICK TEST

1. Why are alkanes called saturated hydrocarbons?
2. Draw the structure of the first four members of the alkane family.
3. Do alkanes react with bromine water?
4. Why are alkenes called unsaturated hydrocarbons?
5. Draw the structure of the first two members of the alkene family.
6. How are large hydrocarbons obtained from crude oil?
7. Why are the long hydrocarbons cracked to form smaller ones?
8. How are large hydrocarbons cracked industrially?
9. What is the catalyst that is used?
10. What is the ethene produced by cracking used for?

10. Plastics
9. Hot aluminium oxide
8. Heated over catalyst
7. More useful
6. Fractional distillation
5. See below
4. Double bond
3. No
2. See below
1. No double bonds

PLASTICS

LOTS OF SMALL HYDROCARBONS CAN BE JOINED TOGETHER TO MAKE ONE BIG MOLECULE.

POLYMERISATION

We have seen how the simplest alkene, ethene, may be formed by the cracking of large hydrocarbons. If ethene is heated under pressure with a catalyst, many ethene molecules may join together to form a larger molecule, poly(ethene) or polythene.

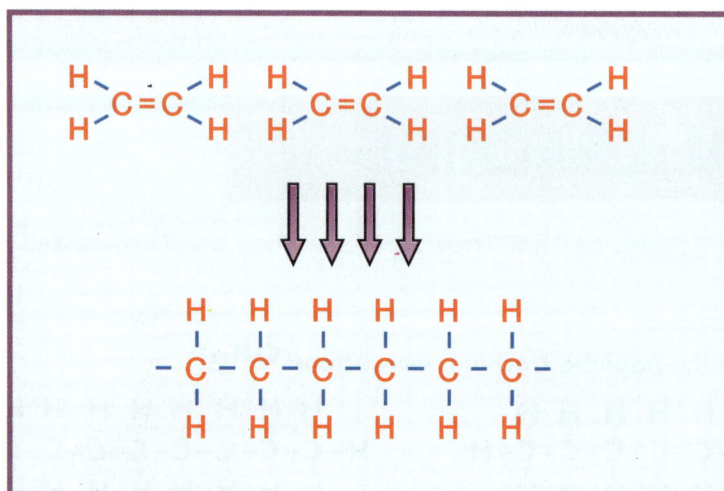

The small starting molecules, in this case the ethene molecules, are called monomers. The double bonds in the ethene molecules open up to form long chain molecules called polymers (poly means lots).
As the ethene molecules have just joined together with no other substance being produced this is called an addition polymerisation reaction.

Examiner's Top Tip
Learn the diagram to show how poly(ethene) is formed from ethene.

OTHER POLYMERS
Polymerisation reactions may involve other monomer molecules and they can be represented as:

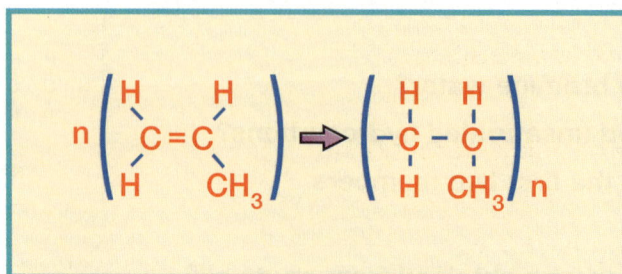

$$n \left(\begin{array}{c} H \\ C=C \\ H \end{array} \begin{array}{c} H \\ \\ CH_3 \end{array} \right) \rightarrow \left(\begin{array}{c} H \\ -C-C- \\ H \end{array} \begin{array}{c} H \\ \\ CH_3 \end{array} \right)_n$$

Where n would be a large number.
The monomer here is propene. It forms poly(propene).

USES OF PLASTICS

POLY(ETHENE)

- Poly(ethene) is <u>cheap</u> and <u>strong</u>.
- It is used for plastic <u>bags</u> and <u>bottles</u>.

Examiner's Top Tip
Know the properties and uses of different plastics.

POLY(CHLOROETHENE), PVC

- PVC is <u>rigid</u> and is used for building materials such as <u>drain pipes</u>.
- With plasticisers added it is used for <u>wellingtons</u> and <u>mackintoshes</u>.

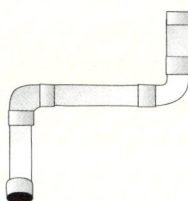

POLY(PROPENE)

- Poly(propene) is <u>strong</u> and has a high <u>elasticity</u>.
- It is used for <u>crates</u> and <u>ropes</u>.

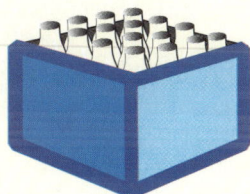

POLY(STYRENE)

- Poly(styrene) is <u>cheap</u> and can be <u>moulded</u> into different shapes.
- It is used for <u>packaging</u> and for plastic <u>casings</u>.

QUICK TEST

1. Draw diagrams to show how poly(ethene) is formed from ethene.
2. Draw diagrams to show how poly(propene) is formed from propene.
3. What are the properties of poly(ethene)?
4. What is it used for?
5. What are the properties of poly(propene)?
6. What is it used for?
7. What are the properties of PVC?
8. What is it used for?
9. What are the properties of poly(styrene)?
10. What is it used for?

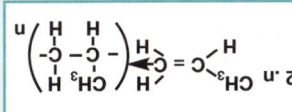
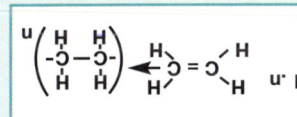

10. Packaging and plastic casing
9. Cheap and easily moulded
8. Drain pipe, wellingtons and mackintoshes
7. Rigid
6. Crates and ropes
5. Strong and high elasticity
4. Bags and bottles
3. Cheap and strong
2. See below
1. See below

15

EVOLUTION OF THE ATMOSPHERE

FORMATION OF THE ATMOSPHERE

THE FIRST BILLION YEARS

- During the first billion years of the Earth's life there was enormous volcanic activity.
- The volcanoes belched out carbon dioxide (CO_2), steam, ammonia (NH_3) and methane (CH_4).
- The atmosphere was mainly carbon dioxide and there was very little oxygen (like the modern day atmospheres of Mars and Venus).
- The water vapour condensed to form the early oceans.

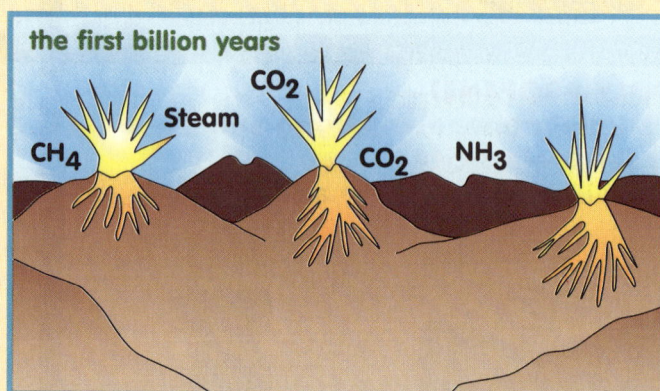

the first billion years

CH_4 Steam CO_2 CO_2 NH_3

LATER

- During the next two million years plants evolved and began to cover most of the Earth.
- The plants grew well in the carbon-dioxide rich atmosphere and steadily removed carbon dioxide and produced oxygen (O_2).

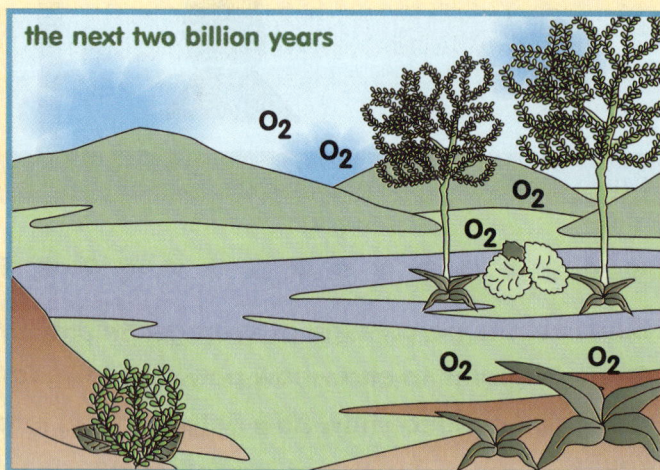

the next two billion years

O_2 O_2 O_2 O_2 O_2 O_2

- Most of the carbon from the carbon dioxide gradually became locked up as carbonates and fossil fuels in sedimentary rocks.
- The ammonia in the early atmosphere reacted with oxygen releasing nitrogen.
- Nitrogen was also produced by living organisms such as denitrifying bacteria.
- As the amount of oxygen increased an ozone layer (O_3) began to develop. This filtered out harmful ultraviolet (UV) radiation from the Sun, and enabled new, more complex organisms to develop.

Examiner's Top Tip
Practice covering up these pages and then try to write the details down.

The composition of today's atmosphere is:
- **about 80% nitrogen**
- **about 20% oxygen**
- **small amounts of other gases such as carbon dioxide, water vapour and noble gases, e.g. argon.**

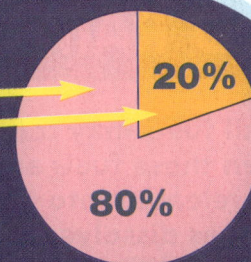

20%

80%

This has not always been the case. Over the history of the Earth the composition of the atmosphere has changed and evolved.

IS BURNING FOSSIL FUELS GOING TO CAUSE PROBLEMS?

- **The level of carbon dioxide in the atmosphere is increased by burning fossil fuels (the carbon in the fossil fuels has been locked up for hundreds of millions of years).**
  Much of the carbon dioxide produced is removed from the atmosphere by the reaction between carbon dioxide and seawater. This produces insoluble carbonate salts which are deposited as sediment, and soluble calcium and magnesium hydrogen carbonates, some of which end up as sediment.
- **Some of this carbon dioxide is subsequently released when carbonate rocks are moved underground by geological activity and become involved in volcanoes.**
  However, not all of the carbon dioxide released by burning fossil fuels is removed by these processes and the level of carbon dioxide in the atmosphere has increased over the last 200 years.

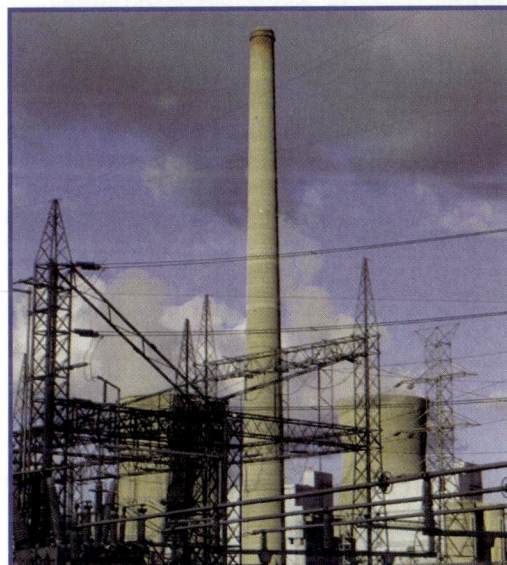

QUICK TEST

1. Roughly how much of the atmosphere is made up of oxygen?

2. What is the main gas in the atmosphere today?

3. What other gases are present in small amounts in today's atmosphere?

4. Which gases formed the Earth's early atmosphere?

5. Which was the main gas present?

6. How did the evolution of plants affect the Earth's atmosphere?

7. What happened to most of the carbon dioxide of the early atmosphere?

8. What does the ozone layer do?

9. How did that affect life on Earth?

10. Why is the amount of carbon dioxide in the atmosphere now increasing?

1. 20%
2. Nitrogen
3. Carbon dioxide, water vapour, noble gases
4. Carbon dioxide, steam, ammonia, methane
5. Carbon dioxide
6. Removed carbon dioxide, produced oxygen
7. Became locked up in sedimentary rocks
8. Filters out harmful UV rays
9. New, more complex organisms able to develop
10. Burning fossil fuels

ACID RAIN

- Fossil fuels may contain some **sulphur**.
- When these fuels are burnt **sulphur dioxide** is produced and released into the atmosphere.
- This gas dissolves in rain water to produce **acid rain**.
- This acid rain can affect the environment, damaging statues and buildings as well as trees and animals and plants.

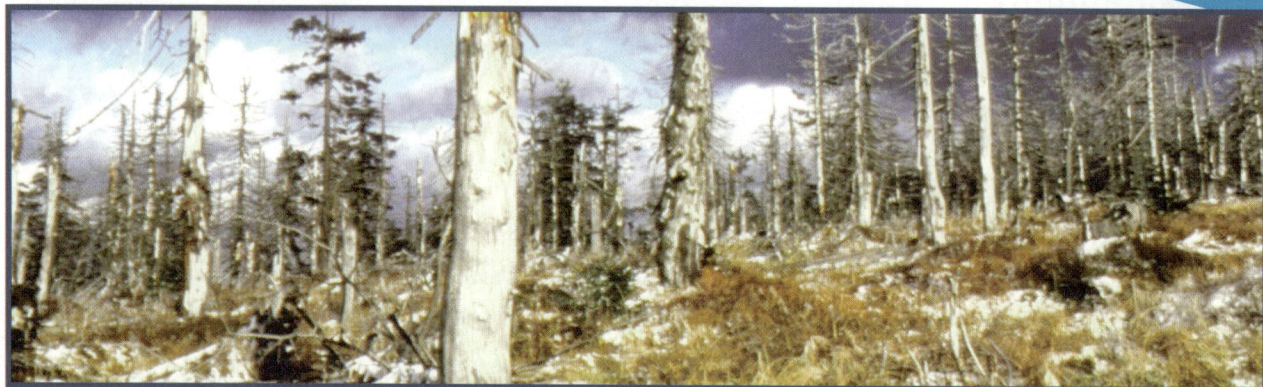

CFCs AND THE OZONE LAYER

- Chlorine is used in the production of CFCs.
- These were widely used in aerosols, fridges and as solvents.
- When these gases escape into the atmosphere they can trigger a chain reaction which breaks up ozone.
- Ozone is a molecule made of three oxygen atoms and is important because it filters out harmful ultraviolet rays. These rays can cause skin cancer and damage crops.
- The ozone is broken down to form oxygen molecules, O_2.
- CFCs have been widely replaced in products, and their production is now very limited.

Examiner's Top Tip
The ozone layer problems are caused by CFCs.

CARBON MONOXIDE

Carbon monoxide can also cause problems.
- When fossil fuels are burnt in insufficient oxygen, carbon monoxide, CO, is produced instead of carbon dioxide, CO_2.
- Carbon monoxide is colourless, odourless and very poisonous.
- Faulty gas appliances can produce this gas, which is dangerous and costs many lives each year.

CARBON DIOXIDE AND THE GREENHOUSE EFFECT

- The greenhouse effect is slowly heating up the Earth.
- When fossil fuels are burnt carbon dioxide is produced.
- Although some of this carbon dioxide is removed from the atmosphere when the gas dissolves in the oceans, the overall amount of carbon dioxide in the atmosphere has gradually increased over the last 200 years.
- This carbon dioxide traps the heat that has reached the Earth from the Sun.
- Global warming may mean that the ice at the North and South Poles will melt and cause massive flooding.

layer of CO_2

heat radiation reflected back to the Earth

light energy from the Sun

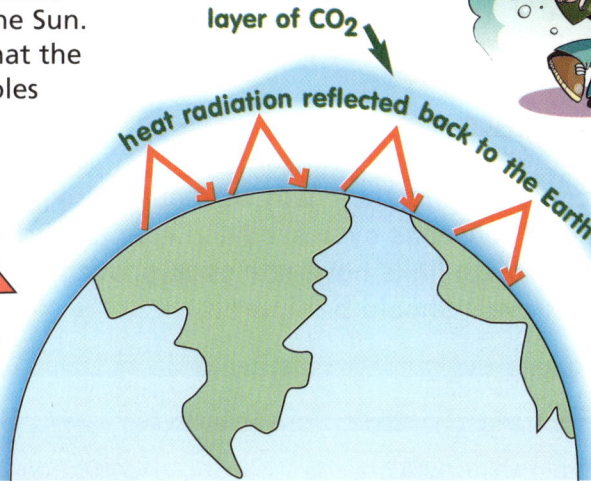

Examiner's Top Tip
The greenhouse effect is caused by carbon dioxide.

POLLUTION OF THE ATMOSPHERE

The atmosphere is being polluted in many ways.

QUICK TEST

1. What is formed when the sulphur in fossil fuels is burnt?
2. What does this form when it dissolves in rain water?
3. What environmental problems can this cause?
4. What gas is formed when fossil fuels are burnt in insufficient oxygen?
5. Why has this gas proved so deadly?
6. What sort of appliances can produce it?
7. What could be the effect of global warming on the environment?
8. Which products contained CFCs?
9. What effect have CFCs had on the ozone layer?
10. Why is the ozone layer important?

Examiner's Top Tip
Acid rain is caused by sulphur dioxide.

1. Sulphur dioxide
2. Acid rain
3. Damage to statues and buildings, trees, animals and plants.
4. Carbon monoxide
5. Colourless and odourless and very poisonous
6. Faulty gas appliances
7. Massive flooding
8. Aerosols, fridges and solvents
9. Break down ozone to oxygen molecules
10. Filters out harmful UV rays

PROBLEMS WITH NITRATE FERTILISERS

Nitrate fertilisers can cause problems if they are washed into streams or lakes.
Algae (small plants) thrive on the fertilisers and grow extremely well.
When the algae die, bacteria start breaking down (or decomposing) the algae.
As the bacteria feed off the algae they use up all the oxygen in the water. Fish and other animals cannot get enough oxygen and die.
This is called eutrophication.

Nitrate fertilisers can also find their way into our drinking water. There have been concerns over stomach cancer and 'blue baby' disease. Although links have not been proven, it seems wise that their levels should be limited.

eutrophication

POLLUTION OF THE ENVIRONMENT

OIL SPILLS

Oil is an extremely important material. It is transported around the world in giant oil tankers. However, when accidents occasionally happen crude oil can escape.
The oil forms a slick which can devastate animal and plant life.

PROBLEMS WITH LIMESTONE QUARRYING

- Limestone is a very important raw material in industry.
- However the economic benefits of quarrying for limestone have to be balanced against social and environmental issues.
- Limestone must be blasted from hill sides in huge quantities which scars the landscape and affects wildlife.
- Transporting the limestone from the quarry can also cause problems.
- However, quarrying does also create new jobs and it brings money into the area.

PROBLEMS DISPOSING OF PLASTIC

POLLUTION OF THE ENVIRONMENT

Plastics are <u>unreactive</u>.
Most do not react with water, oxygen or other chemicals, nor do they get <u>broken down</u> by <u>micro-organisms</u>. This makes them very useful.
Unfortunately when the plastic is no longer wanted, it does <u>not rot away</u>.
For this reason plastics are called <u>non-biodegradable</u>.
They remain in the environment and can cause problems.
Getting rid of plastics by burning also has problems.
Although some plastics burn quite easily, the gases that are given off can be <u>harmful</u>.
The plastic PVC releases the gas hydrogen chloride when it is burned.
In response to these problems some <u>biodegradable plastics</u> have been developed which will <u>rot away</u>.

Examiner's Top Tip
Practice writing these points as 'mini-essay' style answers.

QUICK TEST

1. What are nitrates used for?

2. What will happen to algae if nitrates are present?

3. What happens when the algae die?

4. What is the name given to this chain of events?

5. Nitrates in drinking water have been linked to which health problems?

6. What are the arguments for and against limestone quarrying?

7. Why are plastics non-biodegradable?

8. Why should plastics not just be burnt?

9. What has been developed in response to these problems?

10. How do oil slicks occur and what effects do they have?

Examiner's Top Tip
What can be done to limit the effects of these problems?

1. Fertilisers
2. Grow well
3. Bacteria decompose them, use up oxygen, fish etc. die
4. Eutrophication
5. Stomach cancer, 'blue baby' disease
6. For – new jobs, money. Against – environmental problems.
7. Do not break down in the environment
8. Give off harmful gases
9. Biodegradable plastics
10. Tankers in accidents, oil slicks can devastate animals and plant life

STRUCTURE OF THE EARTH AND PLATE TECTONICS

STRUCTURE OF THE EARTH

- Scientists believe that the Earth has a **layered** structure.
- The outer layer or **crust** is very thin. The crust has a low density.
- The next layer down is called the **mantle**. It extends almost half-way to the centre of the Earth. The rock is mainly solid, but small amounts behave like a viscous fluid and can slowly flow.
- The **core** has two parts; the outer core is **liquid** while the inner core, due to the high pressure, is **solid**.

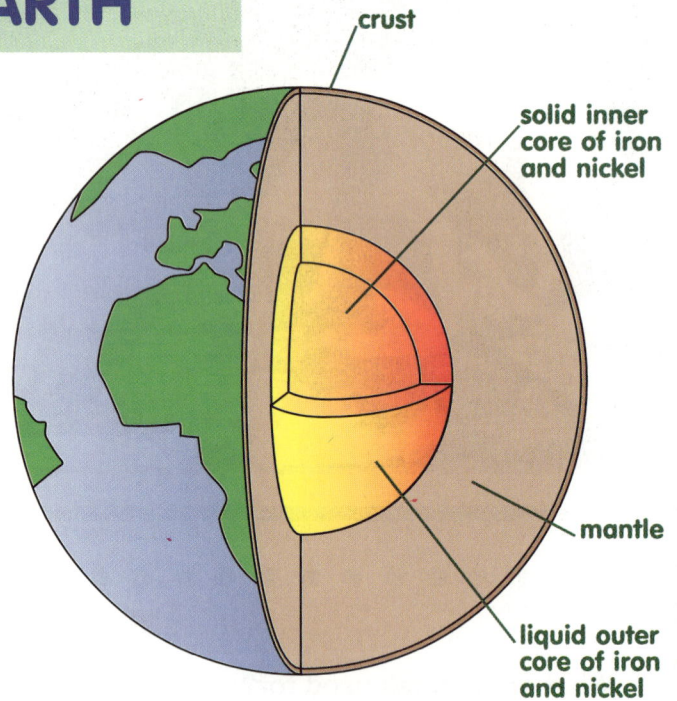

crust

solid inner core of iron and nickel

mantle

liquid outer core of iron and nickel

EVIDENCE OF THE STRUCTURE OF THE EARTH

Evidence for the layered structure of the Earth comes from examination of the paths of seismic waves (the shock waves sent out by earthquakes). The speed of the waves is affected by the rock they travel through. These studies show that the outer core is liquid.

The overall density of the Earth is greater than the density of the rocks of the crust.

This means that the rocks below the crust must be much denser. We believe these rocks are rich in nickel and iron.

Definitions

Core – The core is the central part of the Earth. It is thought to be made of iron and nickel.
Mantle – The mantle is the main bulk of the Earth and is found between the crust and the core.
Crust – The crust is the outermost layer of the lithosphere.
Continental crust – is mainly made of granite. Oceanic crust is mainly basalt.

MOVEMENT OF THE CRUST

how the continents once looked

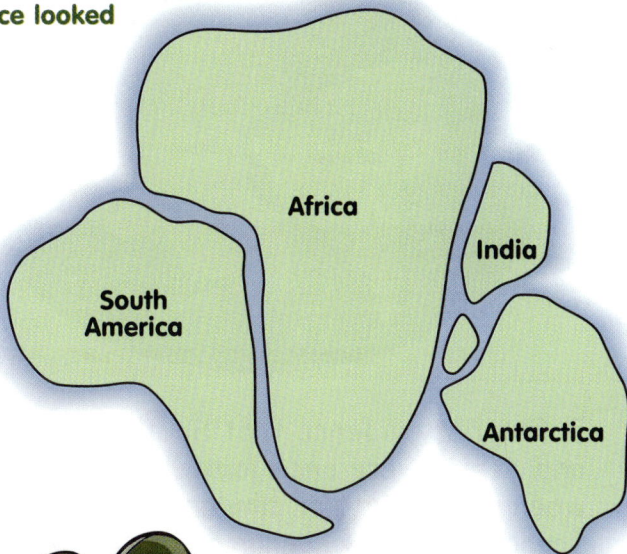

Africa

India

South America

Antarctica

People used to believe that features of the Earth's surface, for example mountain ranges, were formed as the Earth's surface shrank as it cooled. Scientists now believe that all of the geological features of the Earth can be accounted for by a single, unifying theory: plate tectonics.

The main idea in plate tectonics is that the Earth's lithosphere, the crust and the upper part of the mantle, is split into 12 large plates. Each plate moves at a few centimetres per year. The movement is driven by convection currents in the mantle, caused by natural radioactive decay releasing heat.

At one time all the continents were formed into one super continent, called Pangea. Since then the continents have split apart.

QUICK TEST

1. What name is given to the outer layer of the Earth?

2. Which layer is directly below this?

3. What state is this in (solid/liquid/gas)?

4. How do seismic waves give information about the Earth's structure?

5. Why do we believe the core is rich in nickel and iron?

6. How did people used to believe that mountains were formed?

7. What is the name given to the theory which now accounts for geological features?

8. What is the Earth's lithosphere?

9. At what rate do the Earth's plates move?

10. What produces the heat that drives the plates' movements?

Examiner's Top Tip
Practice writing this out until you can remember it all.

1. Crust
2. Mantle
3. Mainly solid, a little is liquid
4. Speed of waves affected by rocks
5. It is dense.
6. Shrinkage of crust
7. Plate tectonics
8. Crust and upper part of mantle
9. Few cm per year
10. Radioactive decay

EVIDENCE FOR PLATE TECTONICS

There are many clues that give evidence about plate tectonics:

1. As soon as the American coast was mapped people began to notice how the South American and African coasts fitted together like pieces of a jigsaw.

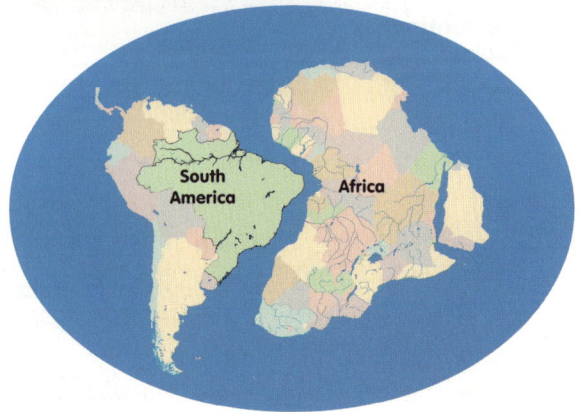

2. Examination of fossil remains in South America and Africa shows that rocks of the same age contained the fossils of a freshwater crocodile-type creature.

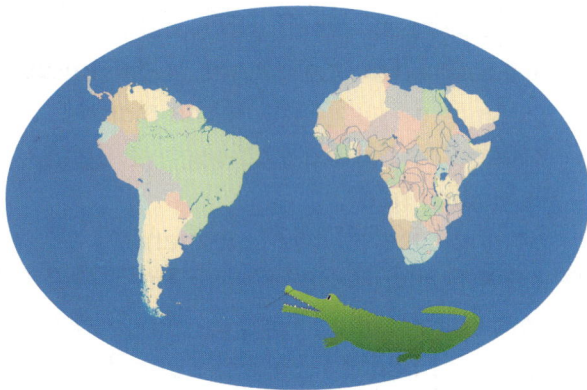

3. Further evidence that South America and Africa were once joined was found when rock strata of similar ages were found to be very similar on both sides of the Atlantic.

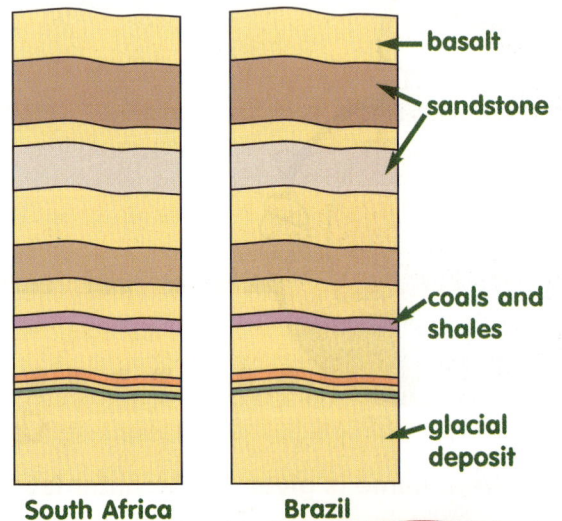

4. Rocks in Britain from the Carboniferous period (300 million years ago) formed in tropical swamps. 200 million years later Britain was covered by deserts. This shows Britain has moved through different climatic zones as the tectonic plate Britain is on has moved.

PLATE MOVEMENTS

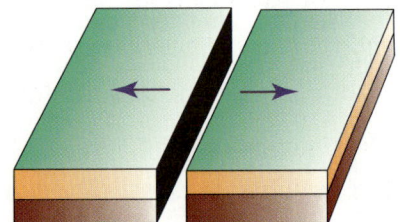

The plates can move in three different ways.
- They can slide past each other (transverse plate boundary or conservative plate boundary).
- They can move towards each other (destructive plate boundary or convergent plate boundary).
- They can move away from each other (constructive plate boundary or divergent plate boundary).

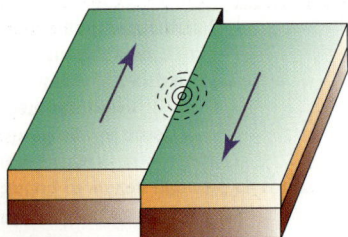

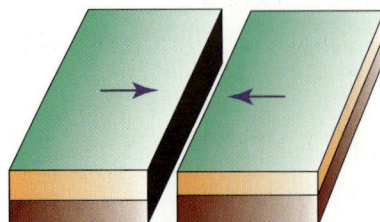

conservative   destructive   constructive

Examiner's Top Tip
Practice explaining the evidence for plate tectonics and the magnetic reversal patterns in a 'mini-essay' style.

DIVERGENT/CONSTRUCTIVE PLATE BOUNDARIES

symmetrical undersea mountains made of basalt

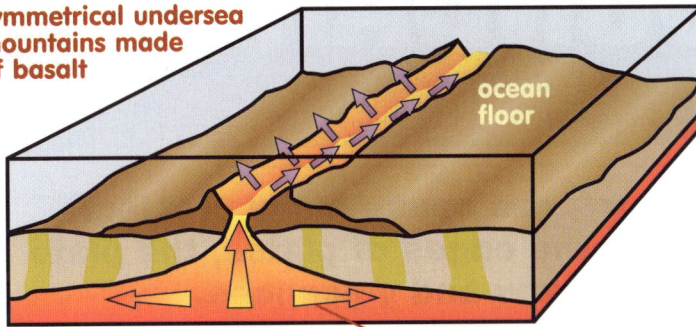

ocean floor

magma

oceanic plates moving apart

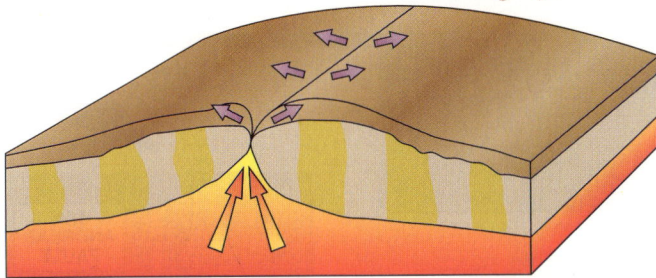

magma

As tectonic plates move apart (normally under the ocean) magma will come to the surface. As the molten rock cools it solidifies and forms basalt, an igneous rock. Divergent plate boundaries are also called constructive plate boundaries because new crust is made.

Basalt is rich in iron which is magnetic. As the basalt cools the iron rich minerals in the basalt line up with the magnetic field of the Earth.

Roughly every half a million years the Earth's magnetic field reverses. The iron rich minerals now line up in the opposite direction.

Examination of the basalt rocks on either side of a mid-ocean ridge shows a striped magnetic reversal pattern.

The pattern is symmetrical about the ridge.

MOVING PLATES

Plate tectonics can be used to explain mountain building and the formation of new ocean floor.

QUICK TEST

1. What is the name of the theory used to explain mountain building?

2. What is strange about the South American and African coast lines?

3. How did the fossil record provide evidence for plate tectonics?

4. How did examination of rock strata provide more evidence?

5. What are the three ways that plates can move?

6. Where do tectonic plates normally move apart?

7. What type of rock is formed when magma cools and solidifies?

8. Basalt is rich in which element?

9. What affects the iron rich minerals in basalt?

10. Explain the magnetic reversal patterns found at mid-ocean ridges.

10. As the Earth's magnetic field reverses minerals line up in opposite direction on both sides of the ridge.
9. Magnetic field of the Earth
8. Iron
7. Igneous
6. Mid-ocean ridges
5. Past, towards, away
4. Rock strata of similar ages is similar.
3. Freshwater crocodile-type fossils found in S. America and Africa.
2. Fit together
1. Plate tectonics

PLATE BOUNDARIES

The movement of tectonic plates can cause many problems. These problems are worst near the edges of plates, the plate boundaries, and include earthquakes and volcanoes.

TRANSVERSE/CONSERVATIVE PLATE BOUNDARIES

Earthquakes are caused by the tectonic plates sliding past each other:

The San Andreas fault in California is a famous example. The plates in this area are fractured into a complicated pattern.

As the plates try to move they tend to stick rather than slide smoothly.

Forces build up on the plates until eventually the strain that has built up is released as an earthquake.

However with so many factors involved it is not possible to predict exactly when earthquakes will occur.

When they do occur, they can cause massive destruction and loss of life.

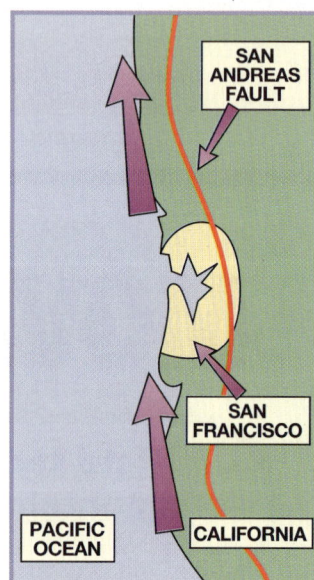

Damage to gas and water mains caused by an earthquake in Los Angeles in 1994.

CONVERGENT/DESTRUCTIVE PLATE BOUNDARIES

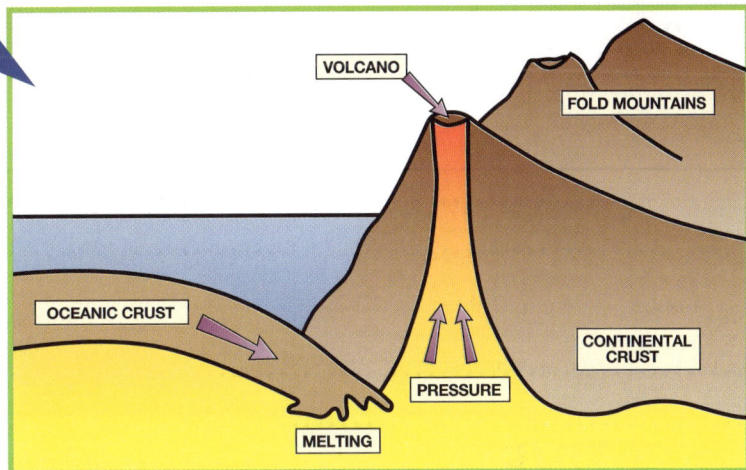

VOLCANO
FOLD MOUNTAINS
OCEANIC CRUST
CONTINENTAL CRUST
PRESSURE
MELTING

- Convergent plate boundaries often involve the **collision** of an oceanic and a continental plate.

- **Oceanic plate** is **denser** than continental plate. At a convergent plate boundary between them the oceanic plate is forced beneath the continental plate.

- The continental crust is **stressed** and folding, and **metamorphism** of existing rock occurs.

- As the oceanic plate is forced down it is **heated** and some of the oceanic plate may melt to form **magma**. This may rise up to form **volcanoes**.

- As the plates are moving past each other **earthquakes** can also occur.

- A convergent plate boundary along the western coast of South America has caused the **Andes mountain range**.

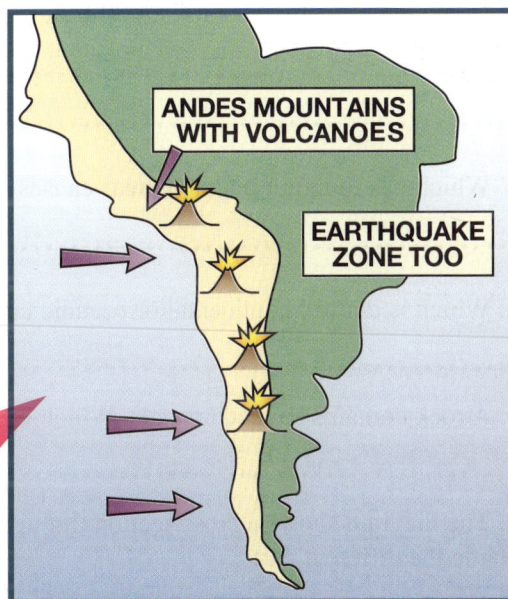

ANDES MOUNTAINS WITH VOLCANOES
EARTHQUAKE ZONE TOO

Examiner's Top Tip
Make sure you are able to draw the two types of plate boundary shown here.

QUICK TEST

1. How are earthquakes caused?
2. Where is the San Andreas fault?
3. Why can't the exact date of an earthquake be predicted?
4. Which is denser, oceanic or continental plate?
5. At a convergent plate boundary is the oceanic plate forced above or below the continental plate?
6. How is magma formed at a convergent plate boundary?
7. What would be formed if this magma reaches the surface?
8. Why are metamorphic rocks found in these areas?
9. Why could earthquakes occur in these areas?
10. Where is the Andes mountain range?

10. West coast of South America
9. Plates move past each other.
8. Heat and pressure changes existing rocks.
7. Volcano
6. Melting oceanic plate
5. Below
4. Oceanic
3. Too many factors involved
2. California, USA
1. Plates sliding past each other

EXAM QUESTIONS –

1. What are the three types of rock?

....

....

2. Which of these three types of rock is granite?

....

....

3. Which gases cause damage to the ozone layer?

....

....

4. Name the gas which comprises 80% of the Earth's atmosphere today.

....

....

5. Which gas found in polluted areas causes acid rain?

....

6. Which is denser; continental or oceanic crust?

....

7. A rock contains banded crystals. Which of the three types of rock is it?

....

8. The diagram shows a cross section through the Earth.
Name the different parts.

a ....

b ....

c ....

d ....

e ....

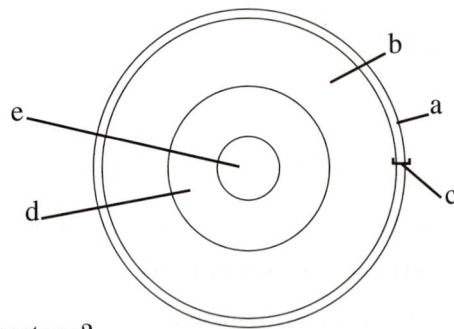

9. What is the name and formula of the main mineral in limestone?

....

10. Give two uses of polythene.

....

11. Name the theory which is used to explain the Earth's geological features.

....

12. Why do the Earth's plates move?

....

13. Give two problems caused by acid rain.

....

14. The diagram shows a cross-section through a rock sequence.
Which is the youngest rock,
and which is probably the oldest rock?

youngest ....

oldest ....

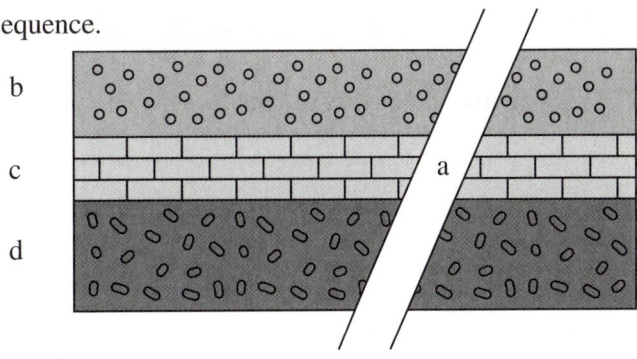

15. A certain hydrocarbon has a very short chain of carbon atoms.
Give two properties you would it expect to have.

....

....

16. Crude oil is a mixture of hydrocarbons. It can be separated by fractional distillation.
a) Which fraction has a boiling temperature of 180°C and is used as jet fuel?

....

b) Which fraction has a boiling temperature of 40°C and is used to fuel cars?

....

17. Name of the process by which many ethene molecules join together to form polythene.

....

....

18. Name these two hydrocarbons.

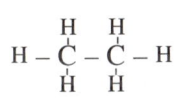

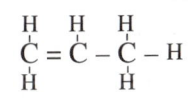

....

....

19. What is the test that is used to distinguish an alkene from an alkane?

....

....

20. The Earth's continents move. Give three pieces of evidence that suggest that South Africa and South America were once joined together.

....

....

....

....

....

How did you do?

1–5	correct	....start again
6–10	correct	....getting there
11–15	correct	....good work
16–20	correct	....excellent

METALS

Three-quarters of the elements in the periodic table are metals.
Metals are found in Groups I and II (the left-hand columns) and the
transition elements (middle section).

Group	I	II											III	IV	V	VI	VII	0
Period																		
1	H 1																	He 2
2	Li 3	Be 4											B 5	C 6	N 7	O 8	F 9	Ne 10
3	Na 11	Mg 12											Al 13	Si 14	P 15	S 16	Cl 17	Ar 18
4	K 19	Ca 20	Sc 21	Ti 22	V 23	Cr 24	Mn 25	Fe 26	Co 27	Ni 28	Cu 29	Zn 30	Ga 31	Ge 32	As 33	Se 34	Br 35	Kr 36
5	Rb 37	Sr 38	Y 39	Zr 40	Nb 41	Mo 42	Tc 43	Ru 44	Rh 45	Pd 46	Ag 47	Cd 48	In 49	Sn 50	Sb 51	Te 52	I 53	Xe 54
6	Cs 55	Ba 56	57 – 71*	Hf 72	Ta 73	W 74	Re 75	Os 76	Ir 77	Pt 78	Au 79	Hg 80	Tl 81	Pb 82	Bi 83	Po 84	At 85	Rn 86
7	Fr 87	Ra 88	89 – 103**	Rf 104	Db 105	Sg 106	Bh 107	Hs 108	Mt 109	Uun 110	Uuu 111	Uub 112	Uut 113	Uuq 114	Uup 115	Uuh 116	Uus 117	Uuo 118

*Lanthanides	La 57	Ce 58	Pr 59	Nd 60	Pm 61	Sm 62	Eu 63	Gd 64	Tb 65	Dy 66	Ho 67	Er 68	Tm 69	Yb 70	Lu 71
**Actinides	Ac 89	Th 90	Pa 91	U 92	Np 93	Pu 94	Am 95	Cm 96	Bk 97	Cf 98	Es 99	Fm 100	Md 101	No 102	Lr 103

Key:
- Non-metal
- Metalloid
- Metal
- Transitional
- Rare-earth element (Lanthanide) and radioactive rare-earth element (Actinide)
- Transactinide
- 'Missing' element

PROPERTIES OF METALS

Metals are good conductors of heat.

Metals are good conductors of electricity.

Examiner's Top Tip
Remember the uses of transition metals and their compounds.

Metals have high melting and boiling points. All the metals are solids except mercury which is liquid at room temperature.

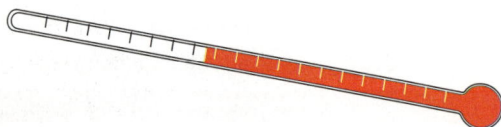

Metals are strong and dense, but they are also malleable (can be hammered into shape) and ductile (can be drawn into wires).

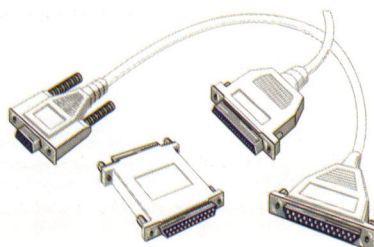

TRANSITION METALS

Examples: <u>iron</u>, <u>nickel</u> and <u>copper</u>
Transition metals are <u>hard</u> and <u>strong</u>.
These metals are much <u>less reactive</u> than the metals in Group I and do not react quickly with oxygen or water.
Transition metals are widely used.
Iron is often used as a <u>structural material</u>.
Copper is a good conductor of both heat and electricity, and it is often used for electrical cables.
Transition metals form coloured compounds which can be used in pottery glazes.
Many transition metals and their compounds can act as catalysts. Iron and platinum are widely used in this way.

GROUP I METALS (ALKALI METALS)

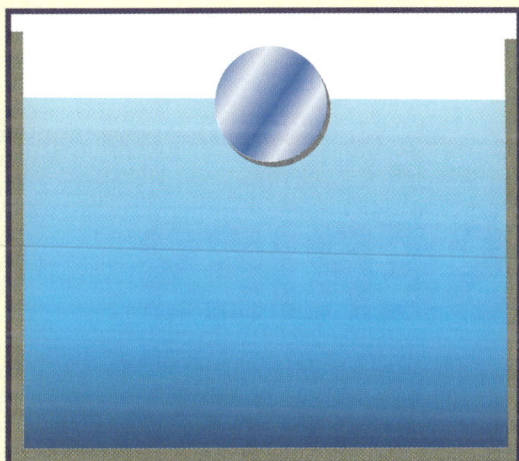

Examples: <u>lithium</u>, <u>sodium</u>, <u>potassium</u>

The alkali metals show these properties:
• they have <u>lower densities</u> than typical for metals and <u>float on water</u>;
• they have comparatively <u>low melting points</u> and are quite <u>soft</u> compared with other metals;
• they <u>react vigorously</u> with water, releasing <u>hydrogen gas</u> and forming <u>alkaline solutions</u>.

The Group I metals react with non-metals to form white, ionic compounds which <u>dissolve</u> to form colourless solutions.

Examiner's Top Tip
Learn the characteristics of metals then cover these pages and write the characteristics down.

QUICK TEST

1. Sketch the periodic table and shade Group I and the transition elements.
2. Roughly what fraction of the elements are metals?
3. Name the only metal which is not a solid at room temperature.
4. Name four properties that are common to most metals.
5. Give three examples of alkali metals.
6. Why do alkali metals float on water?
7. Which gas is released when alkali metals react with water?
8. What colour are Group I compounds?
9. Name three transition elements.
10. Give two uses of transition metals.

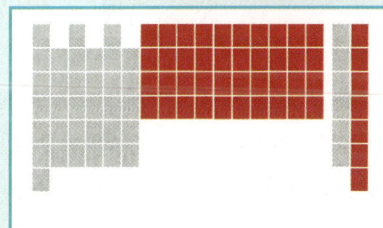

10. Iron – structural; copper – conductors; iron/platinum – catalysts
9. Iron, nickel, copper etc.
8. White
7. Hydrogen
6. Less dense
5. Lithium, sodium, potassium
4. Good conductors, high m.p. and b.p., strong/dense, malleable and ductile
3. Mercury
2. ¾
1. See below

31

REACTIVITY SERIES

Most reactive –	potassium K sodium Na calcium Ca magnesium Mg **carbon C**	Extracted from their ores by <u>electrolysis</u>
	zinc Zn iron Fe lead Pb **hydrogen H**	Extracted from their ores by heating with <u>carbon</u> (coke or charcoal)
Least reactive –	copper Cu gold Au	Metals less reactive than hydrogen <u>do</u> <u>not</u> react with water or dilute acids

This order has been worked out by observing how vigorous the <u>reaction</u> is between the metal and:

- **air;**
- **water; and**
- **dilute acid.**

REACTIVITY SERIES

Some metals are more reactive than others. The metals can be placed in order of reactivity.

REACTING THE METALS WITH AIR

When metals are heated with air they may react with the oxygen present.

metal + oxygen ⇨ *metal oxide*

magnesium + oxygen ⇨ *magnesium oxide*

$2Mg(s) + O_2(g)$ ⇨ $2MgO(s)$

Most reactive –	*potassium K* *sodium Na* *calcium Ca* *magnesium Mg*	These metals react vigorously. They <u>burn</u> fiercely.
	carbon C *zinc Zn* *iron Fe* *lead Pb* *hydrogen H* *copper Cu*	These metals react <u>slowly</u> with air.
Least reactive –	*gold Au*	No reaction

REACTING METALS WITH WATER

Some metals react with water to produce a metal hydroxide and hydrogen.

metal + water $\Rightarrow$ metal hydroxide + hydrogen

sodium + water $\Rightarrow$ sodium hydroxide + hydrogen

$2Na(s) + 2H_2O(l) \Rightarrow 2NaOH(aq) + H_2(g)$

potassium   copper

Most reactive –		
potassium K		
sodium Na	React **vigorously** with **cold water**	
calcium Ca		
magnesium Mg		
carbon C		
zinc Zn		
iron Fe	React **slowly** with steam	
lead Pb		
hydrogen H		
copper Cu		
gold Au	**No reaction**	
Least reactive –		

REACTING METALS WITH DILUTE ACIDS

Some metals (those more reactive than hydrogen) react with **dilute acids** to produce salts and hydrogen.

metal + acid $\Rightarrow$ salt + hydrogen

calcium + hydrochloric acid $\Rightarrow$ calcium chloride + hydrogen

$Ca(s) + 2HCl(aq) \Rightarrow CaCl_2(aq) + H_2(g)$

Most reactive –		
potassium K		
sodium Na	React **violently** with dilute acid	
calcium Ca		
magnesium Mg		
carbon C		
zinc Zn		
iron Fe	**Good** reaction with dilute acid	
lead Pb		
hydrogen H		
copper Cu		
gold Au	**No reaction**	
Least reactive –		

magnesium   zinc   copper

Examiner's Top Tip
The reactivity series not only tells us how an element will react, but it also tells us how a metal should be extracted from its ore.

QUICK TEST

1. How should metals more reactive than carbon be extracted from their ores?
2. How should metals less reactive than carbon be extracted from their ores?
3. How was the reactivity series compiled?
4. When metals burn in oxygen what is formed?
5. What is formed when zinc is burnt in air?
6. Give a balanced equation for the reaction.
7. What is formed when potassium reacts with water?
8. Give a balanced equation for the reaction.
9. What forms when magnesium reacts with hydrochloric acid?
10. Give a balanced equation for the reaction.

10. Mg(s) + 2HCl(aq) —> MgCl₂(aq) + H₂(g)
9. Magnesium chloride + hydrogen
8. 2K(s) + 2H₂O —> 2KOH(aq) + H₂(g)
7. Potassium hydroxide + hydrogen
6. 2Zn(s) + O₂(g) —> 2ZnO(s)
5. Zinc oxide
4. Metal oxides
3. Observing reactions with air, water, acid
2. Heat with carbon
1. Electrolysis

METAL DISPLACEMENT REACTIONS

A more reactive metal will displace a less reactive metal from a compound.

REACTIVITY SERIES

Most reactive –

potassium K
sodium Na
calcium Ca
magnesium Mg
carbon C
zinc Zn
iron Fe
lead Pb
hydrogen H
copper Cu
gold Au

Least reactive –

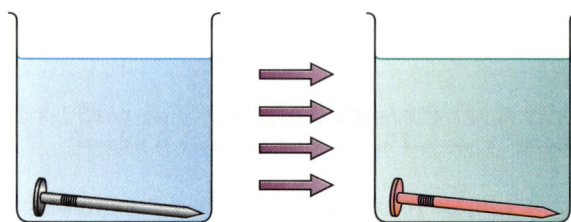

what you observe

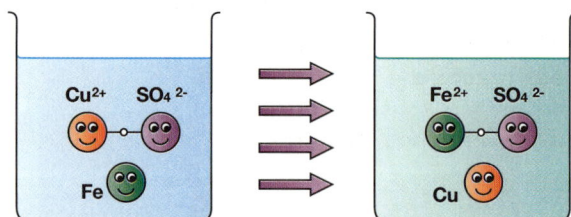

what the ions are doing

- Iron is more reactive than copper.

- When an iron nail is placed in a solution of copper sulphate, the nail changes colour from silver to orange-pink.

- The solution changes colour from blue to a very pale green.

- This is an example of a displacement reaction. The more reactive metal, iron, displaces the less reactive metal, copper, from its compound, copper sulphate.

  iron + copper sulphate $\Rightarrow$ copper + iron sulphate
  $Fe(s) + CuSO_4(aq) \Rightarrow Cu(s) + FeSO_4(aq)$

- If the metal which is added is less reactive than the metal in the compound then no reaction will occur.

  copper + magnesium sulphate $\Rightarrow$ no reaction

Examiner's Top Tip
An understanding of the reactivity series and displacement reactions can help you to predict and explain many chemical reactions.

CORROSION OF METALS

IRON

Iron <u>corrodes</u> or <u>rusts</u> faster than most transition metals.
If either oxygen or water is completely removed then iron will <u>not</u> rust.

Examiner's Top Tip
The rusting of iron has a very slow rate of reaction.

PREVENTING RUSTING

Coating the iron: painting or coating iron in plastic or oil can stop oxygen and water from reaching it, but if the coating is damaged the iron will rust.

Alloying the metal: if iron is mixed with other metals such as chromium it will form the alloy stainless steel. This does not rust.

Sacrificial protection: if a metal which is more reactive than iron, such as zinc or magnesium, is connected to the iron, corrosion will be prevented. Because the zinc is more reactive, the zinc reacts instead of the iron.
The iron is protected at the expense of the more reactive metal. For this reason it is called sacrificial protection. Speed boat engines are protected by attaching a more reactive metal to them.

ALUMINIUM

Some reactive metals like aluminium do not react as quickly as might be suggested by the reactivity series. This is because aluminium reacts with oxygen to form a thin layer of <u>aluminium</u> <u>oxide</u> on the surface of the metal. This stops any more oxygen or water reaching the aluminium, so prevents any further corrosion occurring.

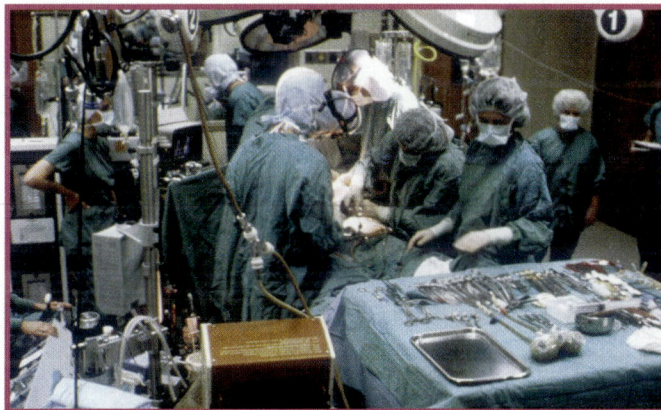

QUICK TEST

1. What is the rule for displacement reactions?

2. What is the word equation for the reaction between magnesium and copper sulphate?

3. Write a balanced symbol equation for the reaction.

4. What is the word equation for the reaction between zinc and iron sulphate?

5. Write a balanced symbol equation for the reaction.

6. What two things are needed for iron to rust?

7. What can be used to coat iron and prevent rusting?

8. How is stainless steel made and what are its advantages?

9. What is 'sacrificial protection'?

10. Why does aluminium not corrode?

1. A more reactive metal will displace a less reactive metal from a compound.
2. Magnesium + copper sulphate —> magnesium sulphate + copper
3. $Mg(s) + CuSO_4(aq)$ —> $MgSO_4(aq) + Cu(s)$
4. Zinc + iron sulphate —> zinc sulphate + iron
5. $Zn(s) + FeSO_4(aq)$ —> $ZnSO_4(aq) + Fe(s)$
6. Oxygen + water
7. Paint/plastic/oil
8. Alloy iron with another metal such as Cr, does not rust
9. Mg/Zn is in contact with Fe, Fe is protected as the Zn/Mg reacts first
10. Thin layer of aluminium oxide prevents any further reaction

METHODS OF EXTRACTION

The more <u>reactive</u> a metal is, the harder it is to remove from its ore. Gold is so unreactive it is found in the Earth's crust on its own (unreacted).

potassium

sodium

calcium

magnesium

aluminium

Metals that are more reactive than carbon are extracted by <u>electrolysis</u>.

carbon

zinc

iron

tin

lead

gold

Metals that are less reactive than carbon are extracted by reducing the metal oxide using <u>carbon</u> (or carbon monoxide).

Examiner's Top Tip
Learn the equations involved in each of the steps shown.

EXTRACTION OF IRON

Iron is an extremely important metal. It is widely used, particularly once it has been made into steel.

THE BLAST FURNACE

The main ore of iron is iron oxide or haematite Fe_2O_3. Iron is <u>less reactive</u> than carbon so it can be extracted from iron oxide by <u>reduction</u> (removal of oxygen) in the blast furnace.

The solid raw materials added to the blast furnace are:
- **iron ore (haematite)**
- **coke (almost pure carbon)**
- **limestone (reacts with impurities).**

WHAT HAPPENS IN THE BLAST FURNACE?

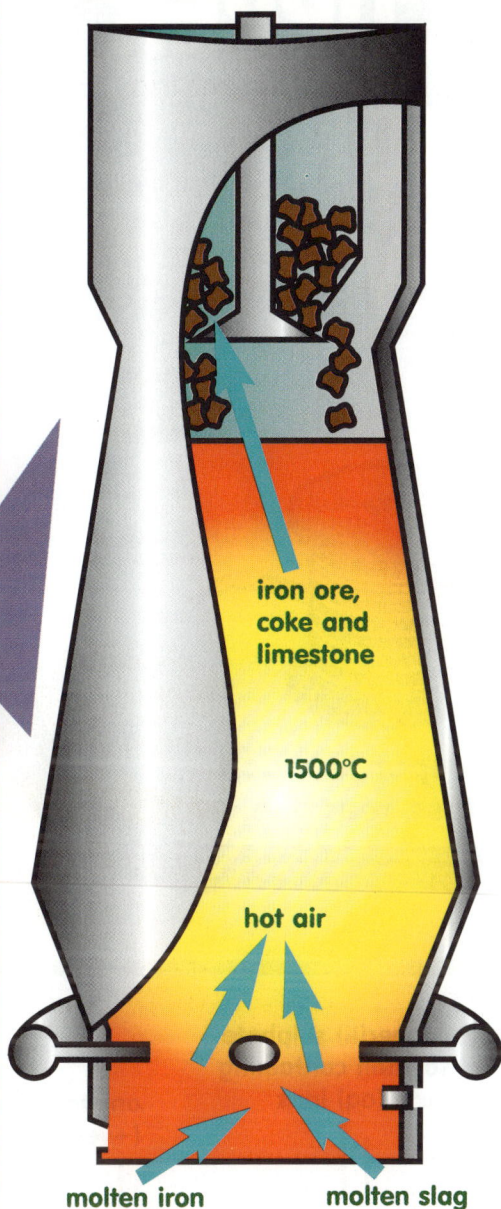

1. Hot air enters the blast furnace and reacts with carbon, forming carbon dioxide and releasing energy.

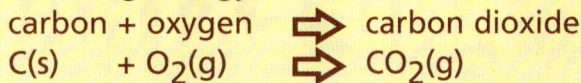

carbon + oxygen ⟹ carbon dioxide

$C(s) + O_2(g) \Rightarrow CO_2(g)$

2. At high temperatures the carbon dioxide reacts with more carbon to form carbon monoxide.

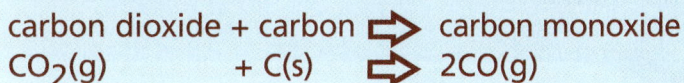

carbon dioxide + carbon ⟹ carbon monoxide

$CO_2(g) + C(s) \Rightarrow 2CO(g)$

3. The carbon monoxide reduces the iron oxide to iron.

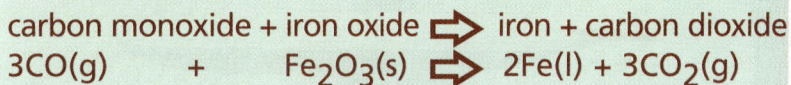

carbon monoxide + iron oxide ⟹ iron + carbon dioxide

$3CO(g) + Fe_2O_3(s) \Rightarrow 2Fe(l) + 3CO_2(g)$

The iron is dense (heavy for its size) and sinks to the bottom where it is tapped off.
The carbon monoxide combines with oxygen to form carbon dioxide, so it is oxidised.

iron ore, coke and limestone

1500°C

hot air

molten iron   molten slag

REMOVAL OF IMPURITIES

Haematite may contain impurities, most commonly silicon dioxide (silica). When limestone is added it removes the silica by forming molten slag. The slag has a low density so floats on the top of the molten iron ore. The slag can be used in road building or for making fertilisers.

Examiner's Top Tip
Remember the iron oxide is actually reduced by carbon monoxide.

QUICK TEST

1. Which element is so unreactive it can be found uncombined?
2. What method of extraction should be used for metals less reactive than carbon?
3. What method of extraction should be used for metals more reactive than carbon?
4. What is the name and formula of the main iron ore?
5. What three solid raw materials are added to the blast furnace?
6. What other reactant must be added?
7. Which gas actually reduces the iron oxide?
8. Why does the iron sink to the bottom?
9. What substance is formed when limestone reacts with silica?
10. What can this substance be used for?

1. Gold
2. Heat with carbon
3. Electrolysis
4. Haematite, Fe₂O₃
5. Iron ore, coke, limestone
6. Hot air
7. Carbon monoxide
8. More dense
9. Slag
10. Road building/fertilisers

37

PURIFICATION OF COPPER AND EXTRACTION OF ALUMINIUM

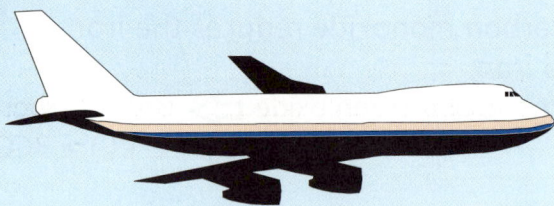

Aluminium is a reactive metal.

Copper is much less reactive.

PURIFICATION OF COPPER

Copper is an unreactive metal so it can be extracted from its ore by heating with carbon. However, the copper that is produced in this way is not pure enough for use in high specification electrical wiring. Electrolysis can be used to produce very pure copper.

cathode (-ve)

copper(II) sulphate solution containing $Cu^{2+}(aq)$ ions

anode (+ve)

Cu^{2+}

sludge formed from impurities

WHAT HAPPENS?

1. The impure copper is used as the positive electrode (anode). At this electrode copper atoms give up electrons to form ions which dissolve in the solution.

2. The Cu^{2+} ions are attracted to the negative electrode (cathode).

3. At the negative electrode (cathode) the copper ions gain electrons to form copper atoms. The copper atoms form on the negative electrode which increases in size.

4. The impurities in the positive electrode fall to the bottom as the positive electrode dissolves away.

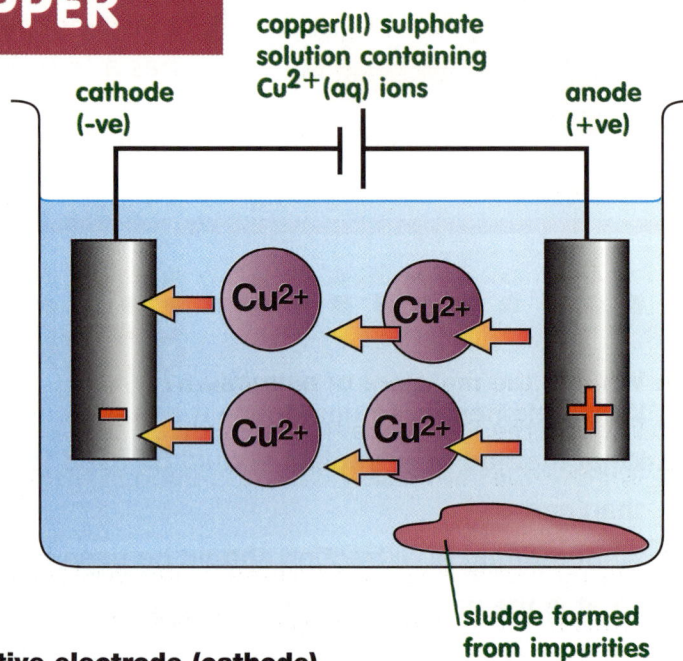

EXTRACTION OF ALUMINIUM

Aluminium is more reactive than carbon so it must be extracted by electrolysis even though this is a very expensive process. The main ore of aluminium is bauxite (aluminium oxide, Al_2O_3). In electrolysis the ions have to be able to move, so the ore has to be heated until it melts or dissolved. Bauxite has a very high melting point and heating the ore to this temperature would be very expensive. Fortunately cryolite, another ore of aluminium, has a much lower melting point. Bauxite is dissolved in molten cryolite.

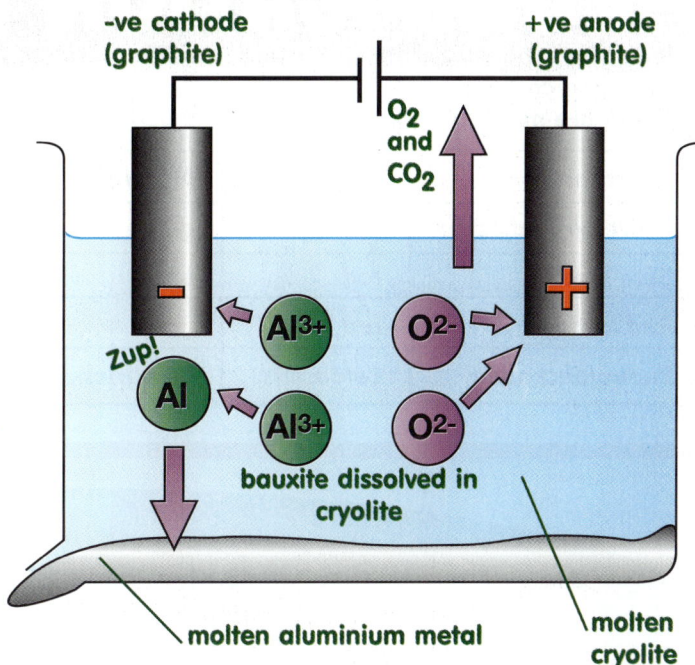

-ve cathode (graphite)

+ve anode (graphite)

O_2 and CO_2

Zup!

Al³⁺

Al

Al³⁺

O²⁻

O²⁻

bauxite dissolved in cryolite

molten aluminium metal

molten cryolite

WHAT HAPPENS?

1. By dissolving the Al_2O_3 both the Al^{3+} and the O^{2-} ions can move.

2. The Al^{3+} ions are attracted to the negative electrode (cathode), where they pick up electrons to form Al atoms. They fall to the bottom of the cell.

3. The O^{2-} ions are attracted to the positive electrode (anode) where they deposit electrons. The oxygen that forms reacts with the graphite electrode forming carbon dioxide. Periodically the electrodes have to be replaced.

Examiner's Top Tip
In the electrolysis of aluminium oxide:
- at the negative electrode positive metal ions gain electrons to form atoms – this is reduction
- at the positive electrode electrons are given up by oxygen ions to form oxygen molecules – this is oxidation.
- This can be remembered by 'oil rig': oxidation is loss, reduction is gain of electrons.

QUICK TEST

1. What is the main ore of aluminium?

2. Why do the ions have to be dissolved or molten?

3. Which other ore of aluminium is used in electrolysis?

4. Why is it used?

5. During electrolysis what forms at the positive electrode?

6. What is formed at the negative electrode?

7. How is copper normally extracted from its ore?

8. Why is very pure copper sometimes needed?

9. At which electrode is the impure copper placed?

10. What happens to any impurities?

10. Form sludge at bottom of cell
9. Positive electrode
8. High specification wiring
7. Normally heated with carbon
6. Aluminium
5. Oxygen, which reacts to make carbon dioxide
4. Lower m.p. and bauxite dissolves in it
3. Cryolite
2. So they can move
1. Bauxite

INDICATORS

- The pH shows the concentration of hydrogen ions [H$^+$] in a solution.
- Indicators show whether a solution is acidic, alkaline or neutral by changing colour.
- There are many different indicators.

Indicator	Acid	Neutral	Alkali
Universal Indicator	red	green	purple
Blue litmus	red	blue	blue
Red litmus	red	red	blue
Phenolphthalein	colourless	colourless	pink

ACIDS AND ALKALIS

ACIDS

Acidic solutions have a pH less than 7. The strongest acids have a pH of 1. The weakest acids have a pH of 6.

COMMON ACIDS ARE:

- hydrochloric acid
- sulphuric acid
- nitric acid

The soluble oxides of non-metals form acidic solutions.

CORROSIVE

ALKALIS

Alkalis are also corrosive.
Alkalis are also called bases.
Alkalis are soluble bases.
Alkalis have a pH of more than 7.
The strongest alkalis have a pH of 14.
The weakest alkalis have a pH of 8.

COMMON ALKALIS ARE:

- sodium hydroxide
- potassium hydroxide
- calcium hydroxide

Ammonia dissolves in water to form an alkaline solution. This can be neutralised with acids to produce ammonium salts.
The soluble oxides and hydroxides of metals form alkaline solutions.

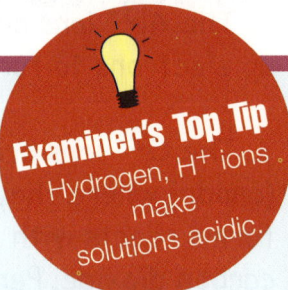

Examiner's Top Tip
Hydrogen, H$^+$ ions make solutions acidic.

NEUTRALISATION

The reaction between an acid and a base is called **neutralisation**.

acid + alkali ⟹ a neutral salt + water

The type of salt produced depends on the metal in the alkali used and on the acid used.

| 1 | 2 | 3 | 4 | 5 | 6 | 7 | 8 | 9 | 10 | 11 | 12 | 13 | 14 |

← ACIDS   ALKALIS →

NAMING SALTS

Neutralising <u>hydrochloric</u> acid will produce <u>chloride</u> salts:
- hydro<u>chloric</u> acid + <u>sodium</u> hydroxide ⟹ <u>sodium</u> <u>chloride</u> + water

Neutralising <u>nitric</u> acid will produce <u>nitrate</u> salts:
- <u>nitric</u> acid + <u>calcium</u> hydroxide ⟹ <u>calcium</u> <u>nitrate</u> + water

Neutralising <u>sulphuric</u> acid will produce <u>sulphate</u> salts:
- <u>sulphuric</u> acid + <u>potassium</u> hydroxide ⟹ <u>potassium</u> <u>sulphate</u> + water

Examiner's Top Tip
Hydroxide, OH⁻ ions make solutions alkaline.

QUICK TEST

1. What is the pH of a neutral solution?
2. What is the pH of the strongest alkali?
3. What is the pH of a weak acid?
4. Which ions make solutions acidic?
5. Which ions make solutions alkaline?
6. How are alkalis and bases related?
7. Name three common acids.
8. Name the salt produced when sulphuric acid neutralises sodium hydroxide.
9. Name the salt produced when nitric acid neutralises potassium hydroxide.
10. Name the salt produced when hydrochloric acid neutralises ammonia solution.

10. Ammonium chloride
9. Potassium nitrate
8. Sodium sulphate
7. Hydrochloric acid, sulphuric acid, nitric acid
6. Alkalis are soluble bases.
5. OH⁻
4. H⁺
3. 6
2. 14
1. 7

METAL CARBONATES

Metal carbonates can be neutralised by acids.

Most carbonates are insoluble, so they are bases, but they are not alkalis.

When carbonates are neutralised carbon dioxide is given off:

metal carbonate + acid ⇨ salt + water + carbon dioxide

copper carbonate + hydrochloric acid ⇨ copper chloride + water + carbon dioxide

$CuCO_3(s)$ + $2HCl(aq)$ ⇨ $CuCl_2(aq)$ + $H_2O(l)$ + $CO_2(g)$

zinc carbonate + sulphuric acid ⇨ zinc sulphate + water + carbon dioxide

$ZnCO_3(s)$ + $H_2SO_4(aq)$ ⇨ $ZnSO_4(aq)$ + $H_2O(l)$ + $CO_2(g)$

MAKING COPPER CHLORIDE

- Copper carbonate is added to the acid until it stops fizzing.
- The unreacted copper carbonate is then removed by filtering.
- The solution is poured into an evaporating dish.
- It is heated until the first crystals appear.
- The solution is then left for a few days for the copper chloride to crystallise.

Examiner's Top Tip
Sulphuric acid makes sulphate salts. Hydrochloric acid makes chloride salts. Nitric acid makes nitrate salts.

METALS

Metals can be reacted with acids to form a salt and hydrogen:

- metal + acid ⇨ salt + hydrogen

zinc + hydrochloric acid ⇨ zinc chloride + hydrogen

$Zn(s)$ + $2HCl(aq)$ ⇨ $ZnCl_2(aq)$ + $H_2(g)$

magnesium + sulphuric acid ⇨ magnesium sulphate + hydrogen

$Mg(s)$ + $H_2SO_4(aq)$ ⇨ $MgSO_4(aq)$ + $H_2(g)$

METAL OXIDES

Metal oxides are also bases; they can be reacted with acids to make salts and water:

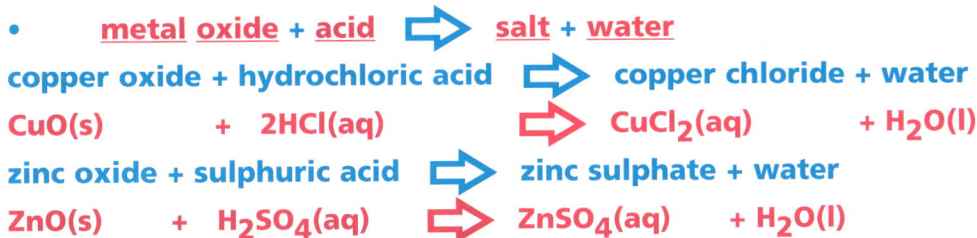

- **metal oxide + acid** ⇨ **salt + water**

copper oxide + hydrochloric acid ⇨ copper chloride + water

$$CuO(s) + 2HCl(aq) \Rightarrow CuCl_2(aq) + H_2O(l)$$

zinc oxide + sulphuric acid ⇨ zinc sulphate + water

$$ZnO(s) + H_2SO_4(aq) \Rightarrow ZnSO_4(aq) + H_2O(l)$$

MAKING SALTS

METAL HYDROXIDES

We have seen that metal hydroxides can be neutralised with acids to make salt and water:

metal hydroxide + acid ⇨ salt + water

QUICK TEST

1. What is formed when hydrochloric acid reacts with potassium hydroxide?

2. What is formed when sulphuric acid reacts with sodium hydroxide?

3. Which gas is given off when carbonates react with acid?

4. What is formed when hydrochloric acid reacts with zinc carbonate?

5. What is formed when sulphuric acid reacts with magnesium carbonate?

6. How could you get a sample of a soluble salt?

7. What is formed when hydrochloric acid reacts with magnesium?

8. What is formed when sulphuric acid reacts with zinc?

9. What is formed when hydrochloric acid reacts with zinc oxide?

10. What is formed when sulphuric acid reacts with copper oxide?

1. Potassium chloride + water
2. Sodium sulphate + water
3. Carbon dioxide
4. Zinc chloride + water + carbon dioxide
5. Magnesium sulphate + water + carbon dioxide
6. Remove unreacted solid by filtering, then evaporate off the water
7. Magnesium chloride + hydrogen
8. Zinc sulphate + hydrogen
9. Zinc chloride + water
10. Copper sulphate + water

EXAM QUESTIONS — Use the questions to test your progress. Check your answers on page 94.

1. Four metals were placed in hydrochloric acid; the diagram shows what happened.
   Place the metals in order of reactivity (most reactive first).

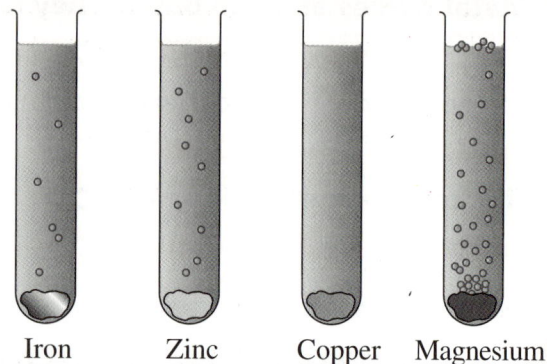

....

2. Give an example of a strong acid.

....

Iron   Zinc   Copper   Magnesium

3. Give an example of a strong alkali.

....

4. What substance could you use to find the pH of a colourless solution?

....

5. A solution has a pH between 5 and 6. Describe what you would see if this solution was tested with blue litmus paper.

....

6. Why is copper less likely to corrode than iron?

....

7. What colour would universal indicator be in a solution of pH 1?

....

8. Put these metals in order of reactivity, most reactive first:
   gold   sodium   iron   zinc

....

9. Copper can be extracted from copper sulphate solution by adding an iron nail. Why does the copper sulphate react with the iron?

....

10. Iron is extracted in a blast furnace. Which solid substance is added to the blast furnace along with iron ore and limestone?

....

11. Name the main ore of aluminium.

....

12. Name the type of reaction when an alkali is added to an acid.

....

13. Name the process by which aluminium is extracted from its ore.

....

14. During electrolysis why do the ions have to be dissolved in water or molten?

....

15. What gas actually reduces the iron oxide to iron in the blast furnace?

....

16. Name the salt produced when:

a) hydrochloric acid reacts with calcium hydroxide

....

b) sulphuric acid reacts with potassium hydroxide

....

c) nitric acid reacts with sodium hydroxide

....

17. Write a balanced equation for the reaction between nitric acid and sodium hydroxide.

....

18. In a displacement reaction a more reactive metal takes the place of a less reactive metal in its compound. The metals are listed below in order of reactivity:

most reactive: magnesium
                  iron
                  copper

The three metals are added to solutions of metal sulphates as shown below. A tick shows a reaction; a cross shows no reaction. There is a reaction between magnesium and copper sulphate which is shown by a tick. Complete the table by adding a tick to show a reaction or a cross to show no reaction:

metal	solution		
	magnesium sulphate	copper sulphate	iron sulphate
magnesium		✓	
copper			
iron			

19. A newly discovered metal is more reactive than carbon. How should the metal be extracted from its ore?

....

....

20. Wasp stings can be treated with vinegar; bee stings can be treated with dilute ammonia.

a) Are wasp stings acidic or alkaline?

....

....

b) Are bee stings acidic or alkaline?

....

....

How did you do?

1–5	correct	....start again
6–10	correct	....getting there
11–15	correct	....good work
16–20	correct	....excellent

SOLIDS

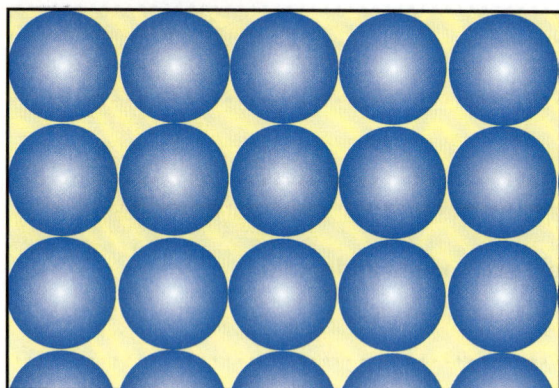

- particles are very close together
- particles are held together by strong forces of attraction
- particles vibrate but have fixed positions

KEY POINT
➡ Solids have a definite shape and volume and are hard to compress.

LIQUIDS

- particles are close together
- particles are held together by forces of attraction
- particles may move relative to each other

KEY POINT
➡ Liquids have a definite volume, but not a definite shape and are hard to compress.

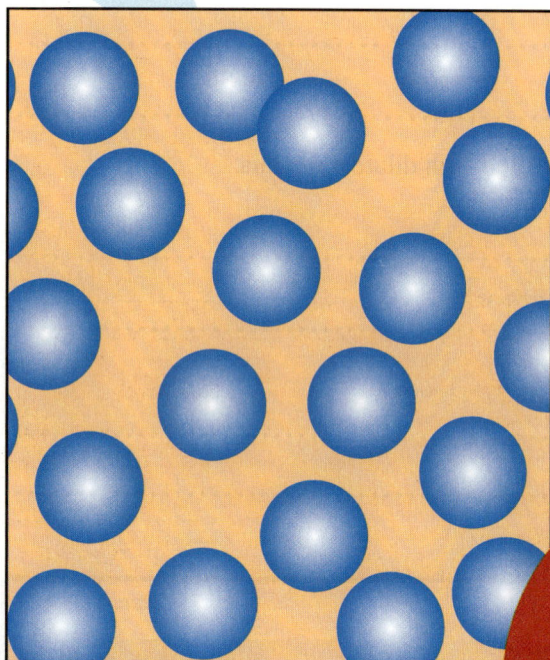

GASES

- particles are far apart from each other
- there are no forces of attraction between particles
- particles may move relative to each other

KEY POINT
➡ Gases do not have a definite shape or volume and are easy to compress.

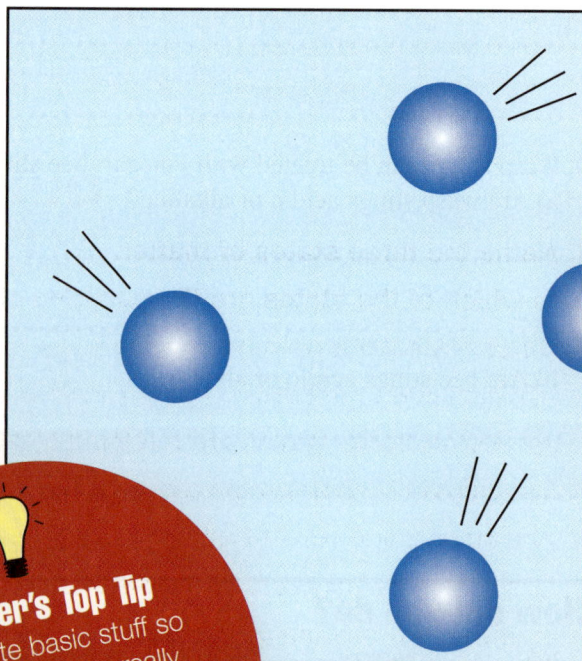

Examiner's Top Tip
This is quite basic stuff so make sure you are really familiar with it. Now draw a temperature time graph to show steam condensing to form liquid water.

CHANGES OF STATE

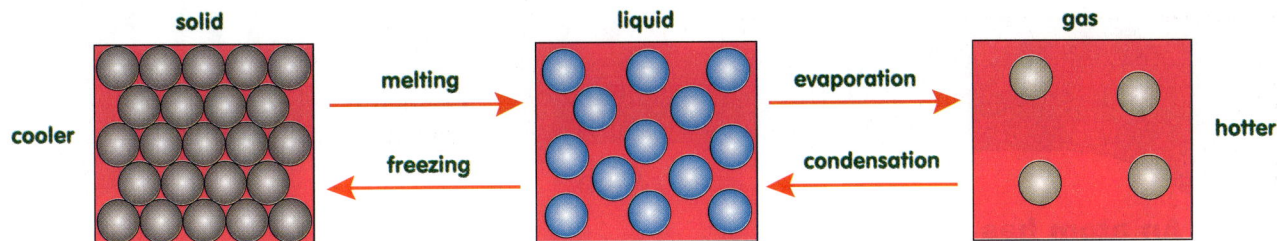

solid   liquid   gas

cooler   melting →   evaporation →   hotter

freezing ←   condensation ←

MELTING AND BOILING

What happens when a solid is heated until it turns into a gas?

- **The particles of the solid are heated and vibrate more.**
- **The vibration of the particles overcomes the forces of attraction between the particles. As the solid melts the temperature remains constant.**
- **The particles of the liquid are heated and move more quickly.**
- **The movement of the liquid particles overcomes the forces of attraction between the particles. As the liquid boils the temperature remains constant.**
- **The particles in the gas move faster as it is heated further.**

water/H_2O

boiling point (100°C)

boiling   gas

melting point (0°C)

melting   liquid

solid

Temperature / Time

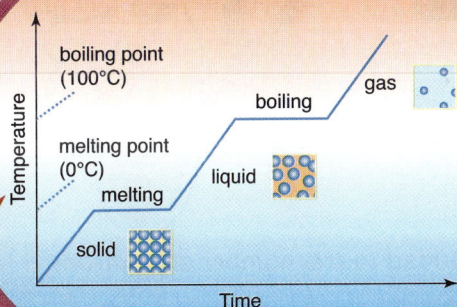

STATES OF MATTER

**THERE ARE ❸ STATES OF MATTER:
SOLID, LIQUID AND GAS.**

QUICK TEST

1. Name the three states of matter.

2. In which of the states are the particles closest together?

3. Do solids have a definite volume?

4. In which state are particles held together by forces of attraction, but the particles may move relative to each other?

5. Can liquids be compressed?

6. Are there any forces of attraction between gas particles?

7. Can gases be compressed easily?

8. In which process do gases turn into liquids?

9. In which process do solids turn into liquids?

10. Draw a temperature time graph to show solid ice melting to form liquid water.

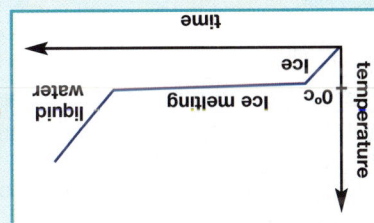

time

ice

liquid water

ice melting

temperature 0°C

1. Solid, liquid and gas
2. Solid
3. Yes
4. Liquid
5. No
6. No
7. Yes
8. Condensation
9. Melting
10. See below

ATOMIC STRUCTURE

An atom has a nucleus surrounded by shells of electrons.

The electrons are found in shells around the nucleus.

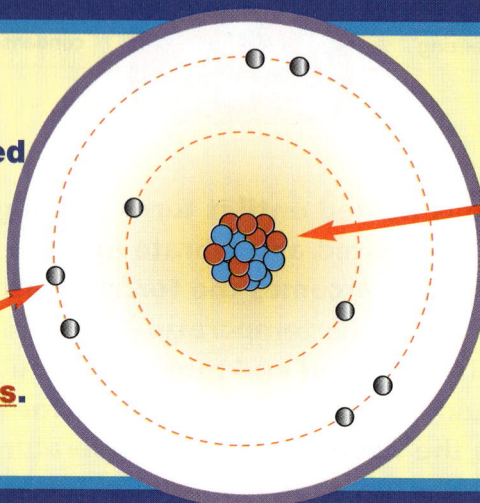

The nucleus is found at the centre of the atom and contains neutrons and protons.

STRUCTURE OF THE ATOM

Protons have a positive charge and a mass of 1.
Neutrons have no charge and have a mass of 1.
Electrons have a negative charge and a negligible mass.
In all neutral atoms there is no overall charge, so the number of protons is equal to the number of electrons.

$$^{23}_{11}\text{Na}$$

the mass number is the number of protons added to the number of neutrons
the atomic number is the number of protons

Sodium has an atomic number of 11, so it has 11 protons.
The sodium atom has no overall charge so the number of electrons must be the same as the number of protons. Sodium therefore has 11 electrons.
The number of neutrons is given by the mass number minus the atomic number.
Sodium has 23 − 11 = 12 neutrons.

Examiner's Top Tip
Be familiar with the charge and mass of the three types of particles.

ISOTOPES

Isotopes of an element have the same number of protons but a different number of neutrons. So isotopes have the same atomic number but a different mass number.

• Chlorine has 2 common isotopes:

$$^{35}_{17}\text{Cl}$$
• 17 protons
• 17 electrons
• 18 neutrons

$$^{37}_{17}\text{Cl}$$
• 17 protons
• 17 electrons
• 20 neutrons

Examiner's Top Tip
In chemical reactions only the electrons are involved.

• The isotopes will react chemically in the same way because they have identical numbers of electrons.

ELECTRON STRUCTURE

Electrons occupy the lowest available shell, this is the one <u>closest</u> to the nucleus. The first shell may contain up to <u>two</u> electrons. The second and third shells may contain up to <u>eight</u> electrons. The electron structure shows how the atom will react.

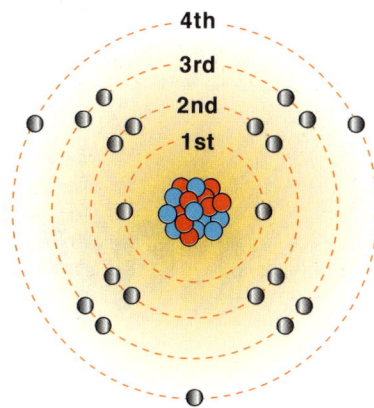

4th
3rd
2nd
1st

a model of electron shells

LITHIUM

*   number of protons = 3
*   number of electrons = 3
*   The electron structure is 2, 1.

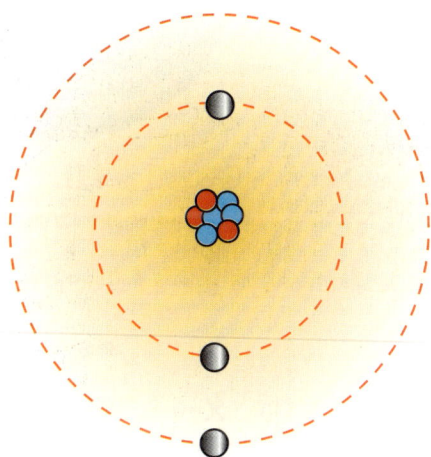

MAGNESIUM

*   number of protons = 12
*   number of electrons = 12
*   The electron structure is 2, 8, 2.

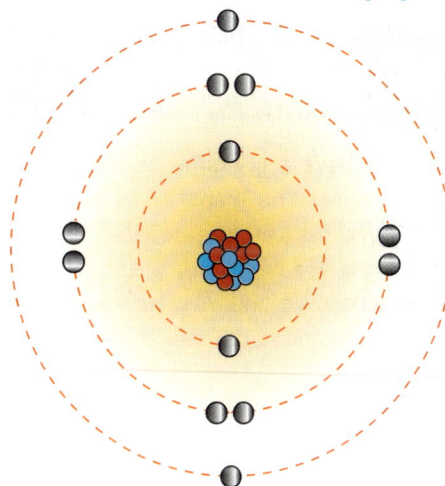

<u>lithium</u> is in <u>Group I</u>

<u>magnesium</u> is in <u>Group II</u>

QUICK TEST

1. What does the nucleus contain?
2. What are found in shells around the nucleus?
3. What is the charge and mass of a proton?
4. What is the charge and mass of an electron?
5. What is the charge and mass of a neutron?
6. What is the mass number of an atom?
7. What is the atomic number of an atom?
8. What is the same about the atoms of two isotopes of an element?
9. What is different about the atoms of two isotopes of an element?
10. Why do isotopes of an element react in the same way?

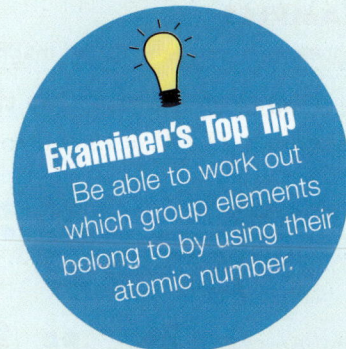

Examiner's Top Tip
Be able to work out which group elements belong to by using their atomic number.

10. Same number of electrons
9. Mass number/number of neutrons
8. Atomic number/number of protons or electrons
7. Number of protons
6. Number of protons + number of neutrons
5. No charge, mass 1
4. Charge −1, mass negligible
3. Charge +1, mass 1
2. Electrons
1. Protons and neutrons

IONIC AND COVALENT BONDING

**Ionic bonding involves the transfer of electrons.
Covalent bonding involves the sharing of electrons.**

Examiner's Top Tip
When drawing the dot and cross diagrams to show ionic or covalent bonding just draw the outer shells.

IONIC BONDING

All atoms wish to have a full outer shell of electrons (like the noble gases).
Ionic bonding involves the transfer of electrons from one atom to another. Metals in Groups I and II, such as sodium and calcium, lose negative electrons to get a full outer shell. Overall they become positively charged (electrons are negative).
Non-metals in Groups VI and VII, such as oxygen and chlorine, gain negative electrons to gain a full outer shell. So overall they become negatively charged.

EXAMPLE
An ion ia a charged atom.

sodium + chlorine ⟹ sodium chloride

The sodium atom transfers an electron to the chlorine atom. Both the sodium and the chlorine atom now have a full, outer shell. Sodium has lost a negative electron so becomes positively charged. Chlorine has gained an electron so becomes negatively charged.

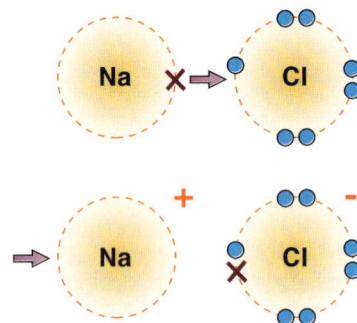

EXAMPLES
magnesium + oxygen ⟹ magnesium oxide
- Magnesium transfers two electrons to oxygen.

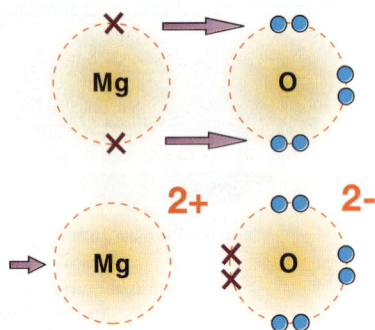

calcium + chlorine ⟹ calcium chloride
- Calcium transfers two electrons in total, one to each chlorine atom.

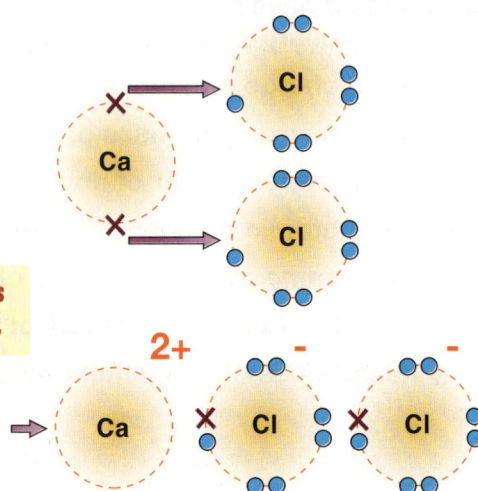

The dots and crosses represent electrons.

All these compounds are held together by strong forces of attraction between the oppositely charged ions.

COVALENT BONDING

Examiner's Top Tip
This is an important section make sure you learn it really well.

Covalent bonding occurs between <u>non-metals</u>. The atoms share electrons in the bond. Covalent bonding allows both atoms to feel that they have a <u>stable</u>, full outer <u>shell</u>.

HYDROGEN, H_2
Both hydrogen atoms have only one electron, but by forming a single covalent bond both can have a full outer shell.

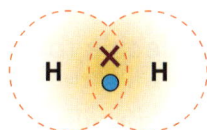

HYDROGEN CHLORIDE, HCl
The hydrogen and the chlorine atoms both need <u>one</u> more electron. They form a single covalent bond so both have a full outer shell.

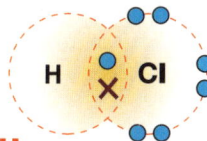

METHANE, CH_4
The carbon has four outer electrons so needs <u>four</u> more for a full outer shell. The carbon forms four single covalent bonds to the hydrogen atoms, so all the atoms now have a full outer shell of electrons.

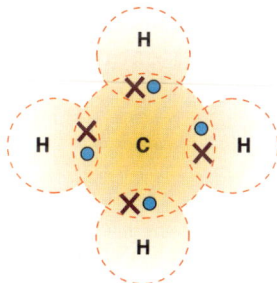

AMMONIA, NH_3
The nitrogen atom has <u>five</u> outer electrons so needs <u>three</u> more. Nitrogen forms three single covalent bonds to hydrogen atoms.

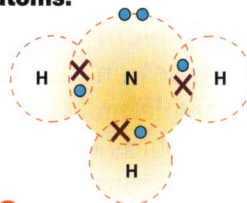

WATER, H_2O
The oxygen has <u>six</u> outer electrons so needs <u>two</u> more. The oxygen forms two single covalent bonds with the two hydrogen atoms to give it a full outer shell.

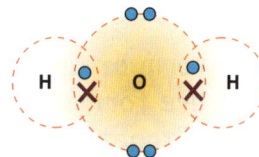

OXYGEN, O_2
Both oxygen atoms have six outer electrons so both need two more. The oxygen atoms form one double covalent bond so that both have a full outer shell.

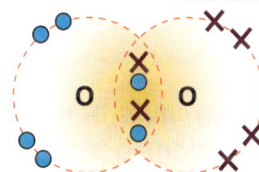

QUICK TEST

1. How many outer electrons do elements in Group I have?

2. How many outer electrons do elements in Group VI have?

3. If an element in Group I loses an electron what charge does it have?

4. If an element in Group VI gains 2 electrons what charge does it have?

5. Draw a dot and cross diagram to show sodium reacting with chlorine.

6. Draw a dot and cross diagram to show calcium reacting with chlorine.

7. What holds together ionic compounds?

8. What sort of bonding occurs between non-metal atoms?

9. Draw a dot and cross diagram to show hydrogen bonding with chlorine.

10. Draw a dot and cross diagram to show the bonding in methane.

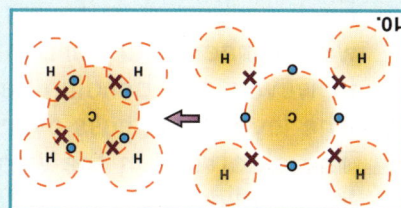

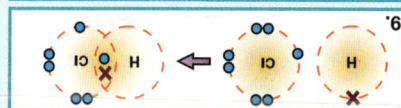

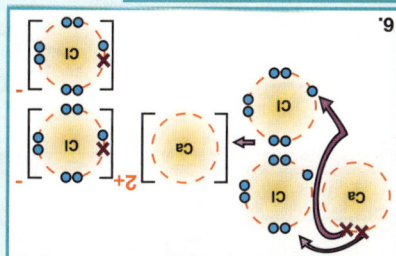

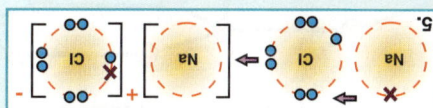

1. 1
2. 6
3. 1+
4. 2−
5.
6.
7. Strong attraction between oppositely charged ions
8. Covalent
9.
10.

51

COVALENT STRUCTURES

Atoms which share electrons can form <u>simple</u> molecules or <u>giant</u> covalent structures.

SIMPLE MOLECULAR COVALENT STRUCTURES
<u>Examples</u>
- chlorine, oxygen, hydrogen iodide and water

These molecules are formed from small numbers of atoms.
There are strong covalent bonds between the atoms in each molecule, but very weak forces of attraction between these molecules.
This means that simple molecular compounds have low melting and boiling points.
Most are gases or liquids at room temperature.
Simple molecular substances <u>do</u> <u>not</u> <u>conduct</u> <u>electricity</u> because they do not contain ions.
They tend to be <u>insoluble</u> in water (although they may dissolve in other solvents).

GIANT COVALENT SUBSTANCES
<u>Examples</u>
- carbon in the form of diamond and graphite

These structures are formed from a <u>large</u> number of atoms. All the atoms in these structures are held together by strong covalent bonds.
This means that these compounds have high melting and boiling points and are solid at room temperature.
Like simple covalent structures, giant covalent structures <u>do</u> <u>not</u> <u>conduct</u> <u>electricity</u> (except graphite) nor do they dissolve in water.

DIAMOND
- Each carbon atom is bonded to four other carbon atoms by strong covalent bonds.
- Diamond is very strong and has a very <u>high</u> <u>melting</u> <u>point</u>.

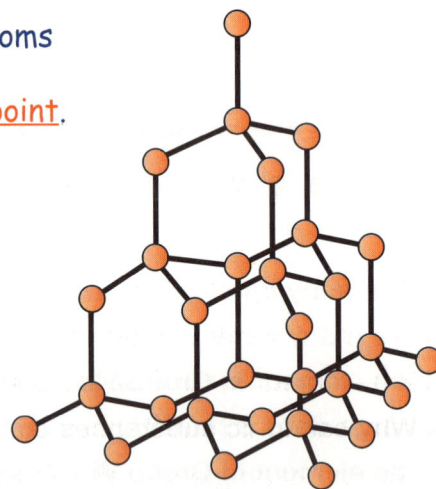

GRAPHITE
- Each carbon atom forms strong covalent bonds with three other carbon atoms in the same layer.
- However, the bonding between the layers is <u>weak</u>. The layers can pass over each other.
- The electrons in the weak bonds between the layers allow graphite to conduct electricity.

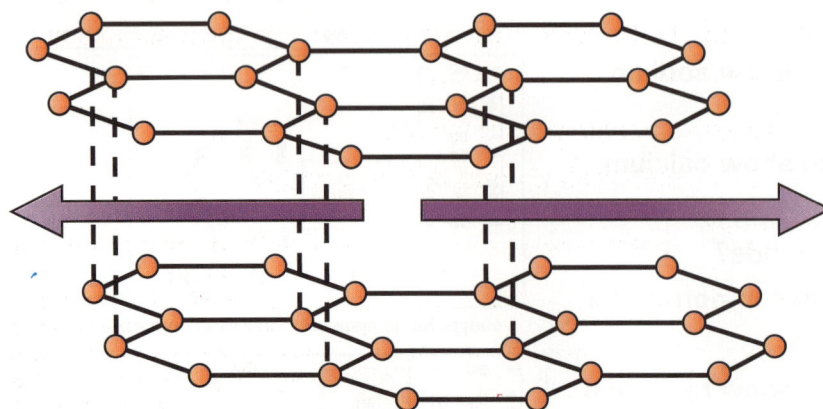

diamond

electricity may be conducted in this direction

graphite

Examiner's Top Tip
Practise drawing the structures on this page.

IONIC COMPOUNDS

- *Ionic compounds are held together by the strong forces of attraction between oppositely charged ions.*
- *The compound has a regular structure.*
- *Ions form giant structures.*
- *The strong forces of attraction between oppositely charged ions means they have very high melting and boiling points.*
- *When dissolved in water to form solutions the ions can move so they can conduct electricity.*
- *Similarly, if ionic compounds are heated until they melt the ions can move and they can conduct electricity.*

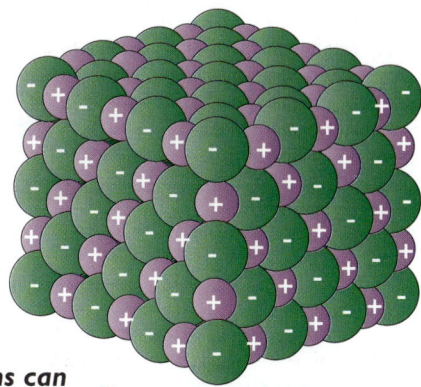

IONIC AND COVALENT COMPOUNDS

Ionic bonding occurs between <u>metals</u> in Groups I and II and <u>non-metals</u> in Groups VI and VII. It involves the transfer of electrons. Covalent bonding occurs between non-metal atoms. It involves the sharing of electrons.

Examiner's Top Tip
Questions on these areas come up very frequently, make sure you know this section really well.

QUICK TEST

1. Which structure do all ionic compounds form?
2. Why do they have high melting and boiling points?
3. Why can ionic substances conduct electricity when dissolved but not when they are solid?
4. Why can ionic substances conduct when they are molten?
5. Give an example of a simple molecular substance.
6. In simple molecular compounds describe the bonding between atoms and between molecules.
7. Can simple molecular compounds ever conduct electricity?
8. Give two forms of carbon which are giant covalent substances.
9. Why do giant covalent substances have high melting and boiling points?
10. Why can graphite conduct electricity?

10. Bonding between the layers is weak and these electrons conduct electricity.
9. Strong covalent bonding through the structure
8. Diamond and graphite
7. No
6. Strong attraction between atoms, weak between molecules
5. Chlorine/oxygen/hydrogen iodide/water
4. Ions can move
3. When dissolved the ions can move
2. Strong forces of attraction between oppositely charged ions
1. Giant structures

53

THE PERIODIC TABLE

As the elements were discovered the early chemists tried to find patterns amongst them, but they struggled to find links.

Group / Period	I	II											III	IV	V	VI	VII	0
1	H 1																	He 2
2	Li 3	Be 4											B 5	C 6	N 7	O 8	F 9	Ne 10
3	Na 11	Mg 12											Al 13	Si 14	P 15	S 16	Cl 17	Ar 18
4	K 19	Ca 20	Sc 21	Ti 22	V 23	Cr 24	Mn 25	Fe 26	Co 27	Ni 28	Cu 29	Zn 30	Ga 31	Ge 32	As 33	Se 34	Br 35	Kr 36
5	Rb 37	Sr 38	Y 39	Zr 40	Nb 41	Mo 42	Tc 43	Ru 44	Rh 45	Pd 46	Ag 47	Cd 48	In 49	Sn 50	Sb 51	Te 52	I 53	Xe 54
6	Cs 55	Ba 56	57–71*	Hf 72	Ta 73	W 74	Re 75	Os 76	Ir 77	Pt 78	Au 79	Hg 80	Tl 81	Pb 82	Bi 83	Po 84	At 85	Rn 86
7	Fr 87	Ra 88	89–103**	Rf 104	Db 105	Sg 106	Bh 107	Hs 108	Mt 109	Uun 110	Uuu 111	Uub 112	Uut 113	Uuq 114	Uup 115	Uuh 116	Uus 117	Uuo 118

*Lanthanides	La 57	Ce 58	Pr 59	Nd 60	Pm 61	Sm 62	Eu 63	Gd 64	Tb 65	Dy 66	Ho 67	Er 68	Tm 69	Yb 70	Lu 71
**Actinides	Ac 89	Th 90	Pa 91	U 92	Np 93	Pu 94	Am 95	Cm 96	Bk 97	Cf 98	Es 99	Fm 100	Md 101	No 102	Lr 103

Note that elements 113, 115 and 117 are not yet known, but are included in the table to show their respective positions. Elements 114, 116 and 118 have only been reported recently.

Key: Non-metal · Metalloid · Metal · Transitional · Rare-earth element (Lanthanide) and radioactive rare-earth element (Actinide) · Transactinide · 'Missing' element

THE PERIODIC TABLE

- In the modern periodic table the elements are arranged in order of increasing atomic number.
- The elements are placed in rows so that elements with similar properties are in the same column.
- These vertical columns are called groups.
- They are often numbered using roman numerals, for example Group I consists of Li, Na, K, Rb, Cs, Fr.
- All the members of Group I share similar properties: they are all metals which react to form ions with a 1+ charge.
- All the elements in Group I have one electron in their outer shell.
- The horizontal rows in the periodic table are called periods. Across a period an electron shell is gradually filled with electrons. In the next period the next electron shell is gradually filled.

THE HISTORY

1864 JOHN NEWLANDS

Newlands arranged the known elements in rows of seven using their **atomic mass**.

Li	Be	B	C	N	O	F
Na	Mg	Al	Si	P	S	Cl

Newlands noticed **similarities** between every eighth element (the noble gases were not discovered until later).
Newlands had identified **periodicity**, but because he left no gaps for the elements yet to be discovered many problems developed.

1869 DIMITRI MENDELEEV

Mendeleev realised that some elements had not yet been discovered. He ordered the elements by their **atomic masses**, like Newlands had, but he left gaps for the new elements that were yet to be found.
Mendeleev was also able to predict the properties of the missing elements. He was eventually proved right when these elements were discovered and were found to have the properties he had predicted. Also, Mendeleev did not stick too strictly to an order of increasing atomic mass.
When similar elements did not line up the order was swapped:

EXAMPLE

Tellurium atoms have a higher relative mass than iodine atoms, but the properties of both elements meant that tellurium was better placed in Group VI and iodine was better placed in Group VII. Although protons had not yet been discovered by lining up the elements in this way Mendeleev had actually put the atoms in order of increasing atomic number, or increasing number of protons.

Examiner's Top Tip
Elements in the same group have similar properties because they have the same number of electrons in their outer shells; this is the basis for understanding all chemistry.

QUICK TEST

1. How did Newlands arrange the elements?
2. Which element did Newlands find to have similar properties to lithium?
3. Why did the Newlands' method develop problems?
4. How did Mendeleev's idea differ from Newlands'?
5. Why was tellurium placed before iodine?
6. How is the modern periodic table arranged?
7. What are the vertical columns in the periodic table called?
8. How many electrons are in the outer shell of all the members of Group I?
9. How many electrons are in the outer shell of all the members of Group III?
10. What are the horizontal rows in the periodic table called?

1. In rows of 7
2. Sodium
3. Left no gaps
4. Left gaps and made predictions
5. Properties
6. Increasing atomic number
7. Groups
8. 1
9. 3
10. Periods

TRANSITION METALS

Group	I	II												III	IV	V	VI	VII	0
Period																			
1								He 1											He 2
2	Li 3	Be 4												B 5	C 6	N 7	O 8	F 9	Ne 10
3	Na 11	Mg 12												Al 13	Si 14	P 15	S 16	Cl 17	Ar 18
4	K 19	Ca 20	Sc 21	Ti 22	V 23	Cr 24	Mn 25	Fe 26	Co 27	Ni 28	Cu 29	Zn 30		Ga 31	Ge 32	As 33	Se 34	Br 35	Kr 36
5	Rb 37	Sr 38	Y 39	Zr 40	Nb 41	Mo 42	Tc 43	Ru 44	Rh 45	Pd 46	Ag 47	Cd 48		In 49	Sn 50	Sb 51	Te 52	I 53	Xe 54
6	Cs 55	Ba 56	57 – 71*	Hf 72	Ta 73	W 74	Re 75	Os 76	Ir 77	Pt 78	Au 79	Hg 80		Tl 81	Pb 82	Bi 83	Po 84	At 85	Rn 86
7	Fr 87	Ra 88	89 – 103**																

The transition metals are found in the middle section of the periodic table.
Iron, nickel, copper and platinum are examples.
All the transition metals have characteristic properties.
They have:
- high melting points
- high density.

They are also strong, tough and hard-wearing and form coloured compounds (e.g. pottery glazes).

COPPER

Copper is a good conductor of heat and electricity.
It can be bent easily and does not corrode.
Copper is used for electrical wiring because it can be bent into shape and is a good conductor of electricity.
Copper is also used for making water pipes because it does not corrode and can be bent into shape without fracturing.

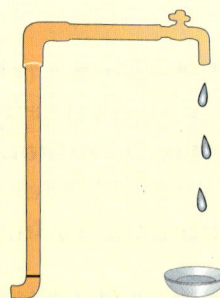

IRON

Iron is strong but brittle.
Iron is often made into steel.
Steel is strong and cheap and is used in vast quantities; unfortunately it is also heavy and may rust.
Iron and steel are useful structural materials.
Bridges, buildings, ships, cars and trains are all constructed from these materials.
Iron is a useful catalyst and is used in the Haber process.
Stainless steel does not rust, but is more expensive to produce.

NICKEL

Nickel is hard, shiny and dense.
It is used to make coins.
Nickel is also used as a catalyst in the manufacture of margarine.

METAL STRUCTURE

The free electrons hold the atoms together in a regular structure and give metals their special properties.

The free electrons allow metals to conduct heat and electricity.

The free electrons also allow the atoms to slide over each other, without breaking. This means that metals can be drawn into wires (ductile) and hammered into shape (malleable).

TRANSITION METALS

Metals have a giant structure. The electrons in the highest energy shells (outer electrons) are free to move through the whole structure.

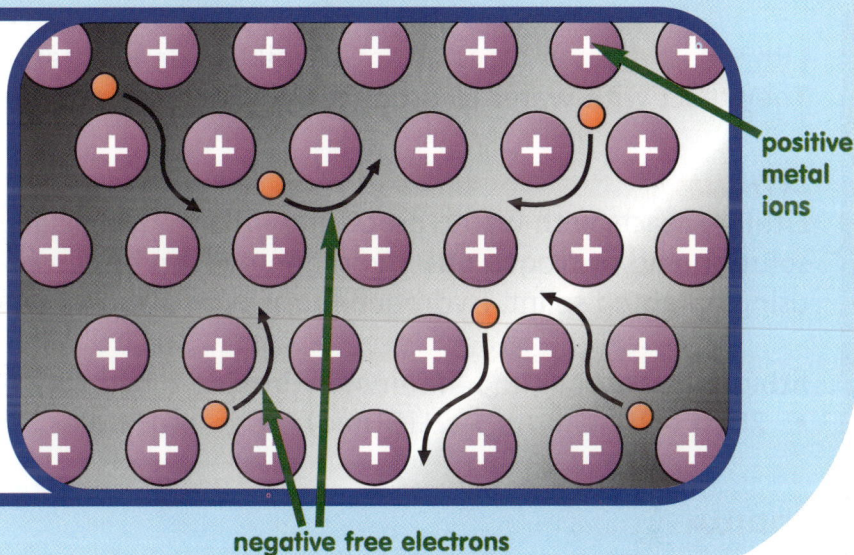

positive metal ions

negative free electrons

QUICK TEST

1. Why are metals able to conduct heat and electricity?

2. In which part of the periodic table are the transition metals found?

3. What are the characteristic properties of transition metals?

4. Why is copper used for electrical wiring?

5. Why is copper used for water pipes?

6. Why is iron often made into steel?

7. Which items are often made from iron and steel?

8. In which process is iron a catalyst?

9. Which items are often made from nickel?

10. Nickel is used as a catalyst for the manufacture of which food stuff?

10. Margarine
9. Coins
8. Haber process
7. Bridges, buildings, ships, cars and trains
6. Iron is brittle.
5. Does not corrode or fracture
4. Good conductor, can be bent
3. High m.p., high density, shiny, tough, hard-wearing and form coloured compounds, catalysts
2. Middle section
1. Free electrons

GROUP I – THE ALKALI METALS

Examiner's Top Tip
Learn the trends down the group.

REACTIONS OF GROUP I METALS WITH WATER

Lithium, sodium and potassium are all less dense than water, so they float.
They react with water to produce hydrogen gas and an alkaline metal hydroxide.

LITHIUM

Lithium reacts with water, producing lithium hydroxide solution and hydrogen gas. Hydrogen gas can be tested for using a lighted splint. Hydrogen burns with a squeaky pop.

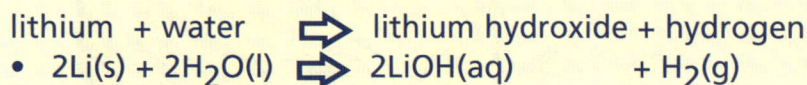

lithium + water $\Rightarrow$ lithium hydroxide + hydrogen

- $2Li(s) + 2H_2O(l) \Rightarrow 2LiOH(aq) + H_2(g)$

SODIUM

Sodium reacts more vigorously than lithium with water. The sodium moves around on the surface of the water and hydrogen is produced. Sodium hydroxide is formed and the solution becomes alkaline. If universal indicator is added to the solution it changes colour from green to purple.

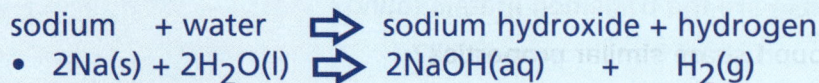

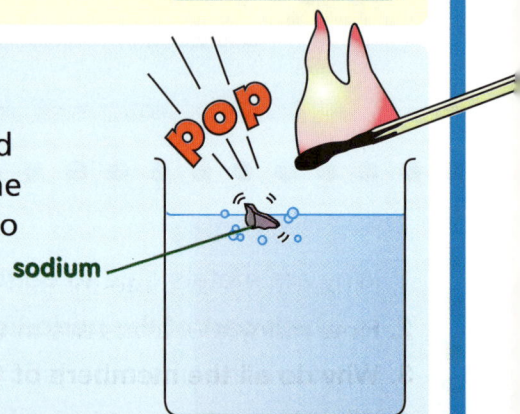

sodium + water $\Rightarrow$ sodium hydroxide + hydrogen

- $2Na(s) + 2H_2O(l) \Rightarrow 2NaOH(aq) + H_2(g)$

POTASSIUM

Potassium is the most reactive of the three metals. The reaction between potassium and water is so vigorous that the hydrogen gas produced may ignite and burn with a lilac flame.

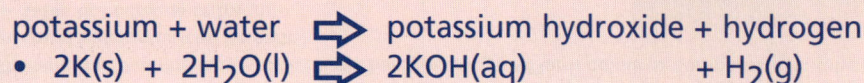

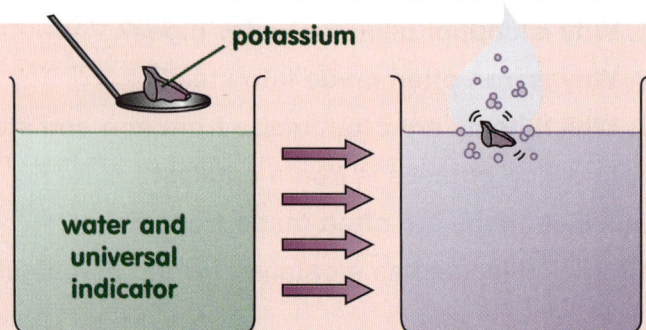

water and universal indicator

potassium + water $\Rightarrow$ potassium hydroxide + hydrogen

- $2K(s) + 2H_2O(l) \Rightarrow 2KOH(aq) + H_2(g)$

Group	I	II												III	IV	V	VI	VII	0
Period																			
1								He 1											He 2
2	Li 3	Be 4												B 5	C 6	N 7	O 8	F 9	Ne 10
3	Na 11	Mg 12												Al 13	Si 14	P 15	S 16	Cl 17	Ar 18
4	K 19	Ca 20	Sc 21	Ti 22	V 23	Cr 24	Mn 25	Fe 26	Co 27	Ni 28	Cu 29	Zn 30		Ga 31	Ge 32	As 33	Se 34	Br 35	Kr 36
5	Rb 37	Sr 38	Y 39	Zr 40	Nb 41	Mo 42	Tc 43	Ru 44	Rh 45	Pd 46	Ag 47	Cd 48		In 49	Sn 50	Sb 51	Te 52	I 53	Xe 54
6	Cs 55	Ba 56	57 – 71*	Hf 72	Ta 73	W 74	Re 75	Os 76	Ir 77	Pt 78	Au 79	Hg 80		Tl 81	Pb 82	Bi 83	Po 84	At 85	Rn 86
7	Fr 87	Ra 88	89 – 103**																

Examiner's Top Tip
Alkali metals are so reactive that they must be stored under oil.

STRUCTURE

The alkali metals are all **very reactive**.

The alkali metals all have just **one** electron in their outer shell.

Because they all have the same outer electron structure they share similar properties.

The alkali metals react with **non-metals** to form ionic compounds, in which the alkali metals lose the outer shell electron to form ions with a 1+ charge.

Reactivity increases down the group (the more electron shells the easier it is to lose an electron).

Melting and boiling points decrease down the group.

Group I	Group II			
Li 3	Be 4			
Na 11	Mg 12			
K 19	Ca 20			
Rb 37	Sr 38			
Cs 55	Ba 56			
Fr 87	Ra 88			

QUICK TEST

1. Name the first three metals in Group I.

2. How many electrons are in the outer shell of all Group I atoms?

3. Why do all the members of Group I share similar properties?

4. What type of compounds do Group I metals form?

5. In these compounds what charge do the Group I ions have?

6. What happens to reactivity down the group?

7. Why does this trend occur?

8. Why do lithium, sodium and potassium float on water?

9. What is the test for hydrogen gas?

10. Give the equation for the reaction between sodium and water.

10. $2Na(s) + 2H_2O(l) \longrightarrow 2NaOH(aq) + H_2(g)$
9. Burns with a 'squeaky pop'
8. Less dense
7. The more shells the easier it is to lose an electron.
6. Increases
5. 1+
4. Ionic
3. Same outer electron structure
2. 1
1. Li, Na, K

STRUCTURE

Down the group the atoms become larger (due to an extra electron shell); they become <u>less</u> <u>reactive</u> (due to the extra electron shell they find it harder to attract electrons).

The halogens have <u>coloured</u> <u>vapours</u>.

Down the group the colour of the vapour gets <u>darker</u>.

Melting and boiling points <u>increase</u> down the group (the first two are gases, the next, bromine, is a liquid and iodine is a solid).

All the halogens are <u>poisonous</u> and should only be used in a fume cupboard.

Halogens react with metals to form <u>compounds</u>, in which the chloride, bromide or iodide ion carries a 1– charge.

They are brittle and crumbly when solid.

They are poor conductors of heat and electricity.

V	VI	VII	0
			He 2
	O 8	F 9	Ne 10
	S 16	Cl 17	Ar 18
	Se 34	Br 35	Kr 36
	Te 52	I 53	Xe 54
	Po 84	At 85	Rn 86

DISPLACEMENT REACTIONS

A more reactive halogen will displace a less reactive halogen from its solution.
Chlorine will displace bromine and iodine.
Bromine will displace iodine, but not chlorine.

EXAMPLE

<u>Chlorine</u> will displace iodine from a solution of potassium iodide.

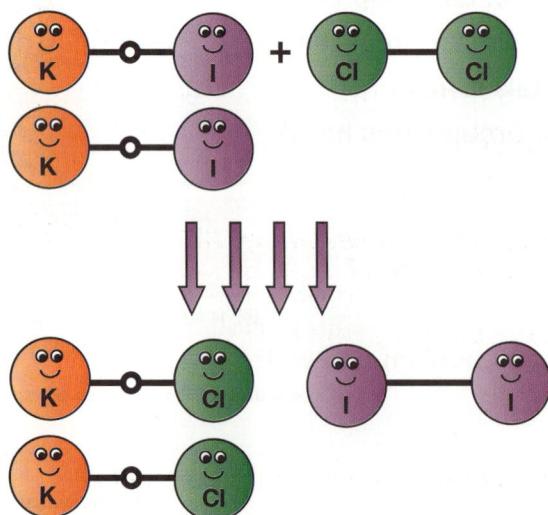

chlorine + potassium iodide ⟹ iodine + potassium chloride

$Cl_2(g)$ + $2KI(aq)$ ⟹ $I_2(aq)$ + $2KCl(aq)$

Examiner's Top Tip
All Group VII atoms form diatomic molecules.

Examiner's Top Tip
All atoms in Group VII have seven outer electrons.

THE HALOGEN FAMILY

FLUORINE
- Fluorine is a <u>very</u> <u>poisonous</u>, pale yellow <u>gas</u>.

CHLORINE
- Chlorine is a <u>poisonous</u>, pale green <u>gas</u>.
- Chlorine is used in water purification and bleaching.

BROMINE
- Bromine is a <u>poisonous</u>, dense, brown <u>liquid</u>.

IODINE
- Iodine is a dark grey, crystalline <u>solid</u> or a purple <u>vapour</u>.
- Iodine solution is used as an antiseptic.

Examiner's Top Tip
Learn the uses of the different halogens.

GROUP VII – THE HALOGENS

The halogens are <u>non-metals</u>.

		V	VI	VII	0
					He 2
			O 8	F 9	Ne 10
			S 16	Cl 17	Ar 18
			Se 34	Br 35	Kr 36
			Te 52	I 53	Xe 54
			Po 84	At 85	Rn 86

QUICK TEST

1. What is the name used for Group VII?
2. What is the trend in the size of atoms down Group VII?
3. What is the trend in reactivity down Group VII?
4. What safety precautions should be used for halogens?
5. What is the trend in the melting and boiling points down Group VII?
6. What is the state of the first four halogens?
7. What is the trend in the colour of the elements down Group VII?
8. What is chlorine used for?
9. What is iodine solution used for?
10. What would happen if chlorine gas was reacted with potassium bromide?

Examiner's Top Tip
Compare the trends for Group VII with the trends for Group I.

1. Halogens
2. Increases
3. Decrease
4. Fume cupboard, etc
5. Increase
6. Gas, gas, liquid, solid
7. Colour gets darker (pale yellow, green, brown, dark grey/purple)
8. Water purification/bleaching
9. Antiseptic
10. Displacement gives potassium chloride + bromine.

THE NOBLE GASES

The noble gases are <u>unreactive</u>.
They are sometimes called 'inert' because they <u>do</u> <u>not</u> <u>react</u>.
This is because they <u>all</u> <u>have</u> <u>a</u> <u>full</u> <u>outer</u> <u>shell</u> of <u>electrons</u>.

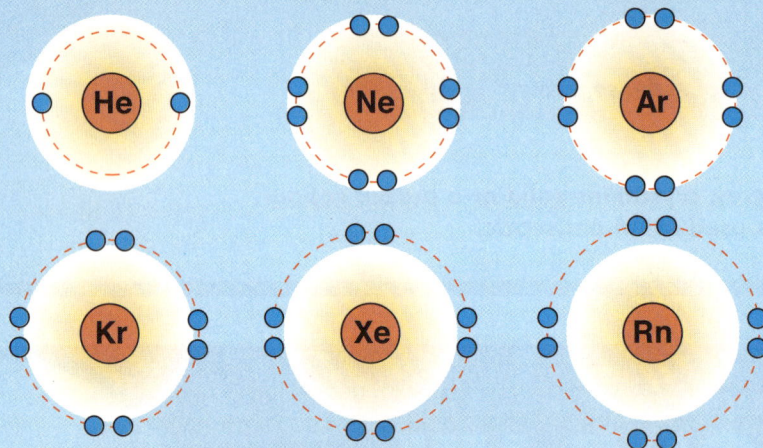

He   Ne   Ar

Kr   Xe   Rn

a model showing the outer shell of electrons

USES OF THE NOBLE GASES

HELIUM

- Helium is used in <u>balloons</u> and in <u>airships</u>, because it is <u>less</u> <u>dense</u> than air (and <u>not</u> <u>flammable</u> like hydrogen).

ARGON

- Argon is used in light bulbs (<u>filament</u> <u>lamps</u>).
- Surrounding the hot filament lamp with inert argon stops it from burning away.

NEON

- Neon is used in electrical discharge tubes in advertising signs.

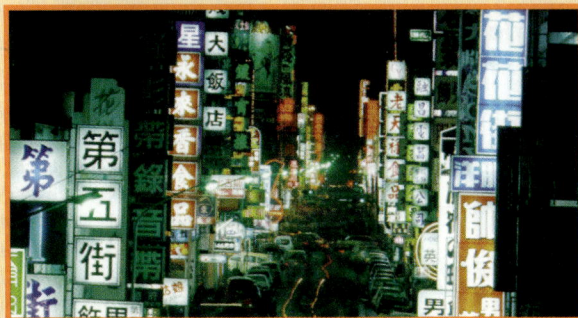

KRYPTON

- Krypton is used in <u>lasers</u>.

THE TRENDS IN THE NOBLE GASES, GROUP 0

As you go down the group:
- **density increases**
- **boiling point increases**
- **they are <u>colourless</u>, <u>monatomic</u> <u>gases</u>** (they exist as individual atoms rather than as diatomic molecules as other gases do).

	V	VI	VII	0
				He 2
	O 8	F 9	Ne 10
	S 16	Cl 17	Ar 18
	Se 34	Br 35	Kr 36
	Te 52	I 53	Xe 54
	Po 84	At 85	Rn 86

WHY DON'T NOBLE GASES REACT?

Atoms react to form compounds by either sharing, gaining or losing electrons so that they can obtain a fuller outer shell. As noble gases already have a full outer shell they do not form compounds.

Examiner's Top Tip
Learn the trends down this non-metal group, and the uses of the noble gases.

Examiner's Top Tip
There is room for up to two electrons in the first shell, and up to eight in the second shell.

QUICK TEST

1. Why are the noble gases unreactive?
2. As you go down the group, what happens to density and boiling point?
3. Draw the (outer shell) electron structure of helium.
4. Draw the (outer shell) electron structure of argon.
5. What does 'monatomic' mean?
6. What is helium used for?
7. Why is it used?
8. What is neon used for?
9. What is argon used for?
10. What is krypton used for?

10. Lasers
9. Surrounds filaments in light bulbs
8. Electrical discharge tubes
7. Less dense than air and not flammable
6. Balloons and airships
5. Individual atoms
4. See diagram opposite
3. See diagram opposite
2. Increases
1. Full outer shell

SODIUM CHLORIDE

Sodium chloride (common salt) is an important resource.

Sodium chloride is a compound of a Group I metal (sodium) and a Group VII non-metal (chlorine).

Salt is found in large quantities in the sea and also in vast underground deposits laid down as ancient seas evaporated.

Rock salt is used on icy roads.

The salt lowers the freezing point of water from 0°C to about −5°C.

This means that the water on the roads does not freeze to form ice until the temperature is much lower.

Examiner's Top Tip
Now cover this page and try to write down the uses of sodium chloride.

ELECTROLYSIS OF BRINE

ELECTROLYSIS OF SODIUM CHLORIDE SOLUTION (BRINE)

Sodium chloride dissolved in water is called brine. Electrolysis of concentrated brine solution is an important industrial process.

Examiner's Top Tip
Learn what happens when a concentrated sodium chloride solution is electrolysed.

chlorine gas

hydrogen gas

$2Cl^- \Rightarrow Cl_2 + 2e^-$

Cl Cl

H H

stay in solution

+

Cl⁻

Na⁺

H⁺

−

Cl⁻

OH⁻

H⁺

+ve electrode

$2H^+ + 2e^- \Rightarrow H_2$

−ve electrode

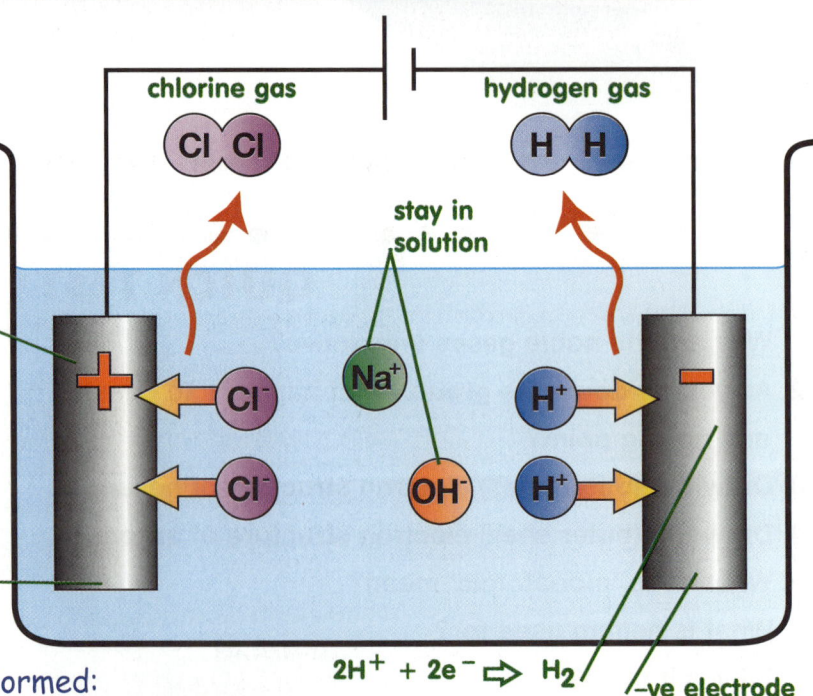

Three important products are formed:
• Chlorine gas is released at the positive electrode.
• Hydrogen gas is formed at the negative electrode.
• A solution of sodium hydroxide is also produced.

Each of these products can be used to make other useful materials.

USEFUL PRODUCTS FROM THE ELECTROLYSIS OF BRINE

CHLORINE

This is used:

- to make bleach
- to sterilise water
- to produce hydrochloric acid
- in the production of PVC

HYDROGEN

This is used in the manufacture of margarine.

MARGARINE

SODIUM HYDROXIDE

This is an alkali used in paper-making and the manufacture of many products including:

- soaps and detergents
- rayon and acetate fibres

QUICK TEST

1. What groups do sodium and chlorine belong to?

2. Where is salt found?

3. Why are roads 'salted'?

4. What is brine?

5. During the electrolysis of brine what is formed at the positive electrode?

6. What is formed at the negative electrode?

7. Which other useful chemical is made?

8. What are the uses of chlorine?

9. What are the uses of hydrogen?

10. What are the uses of sodium hydroxide?

10. Soap, detergents, paper, rayon, acetate
9. Manufacture margarine
8. Bleach, sterilise water, hydrochloric acid, PVC
7. Sodium hydroxide
6. Hydrogen
5. Chlorine
4. Sodium chloride dissolved in water
3. Salt lowers the freezing point of water.
2. Sea, underground deposits
1. I and VII

1. The three boxes show the particle arrangements in a solid, liquid and a gas.
   Which diagram represents which state of matter?

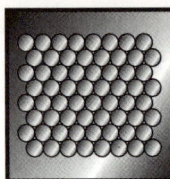

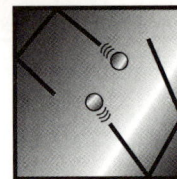

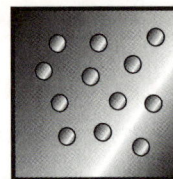

   ....

   ....

   ....

   a   b   c

2. What is the charge on a proton?

   ....

3. What is the chemical formula of sodium chloride?

   ....

4. What is the name given to the vertical columns in the periodic table?

   ....

5. Name three elements from Group I.

   ....

6. Name three elements from Group VII.

   ....

7. Name three elements from Group 0.

   ....

8. a) In which group of the periodic table is this element found?

   ....

   b) How many protons does an atom of this element have?

   ....

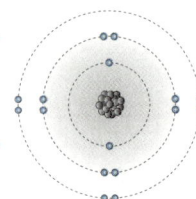

9. Can covalent compounds conduct electricity?

   ....

   ....

10. How are the elements arranged in the periodic table?

    ....

    ....

11. An element has seven electrons. What is its electronic structure and to which group does it belong?

    ....

12. Sodium is in Group I of the periodic table. What does this tell you about the electronic structure of sodium?

    ....

    ....

13. fluorine – chlorine – bromine – iodine
These four elements belong to Group VII; which one is a liquid at room temperature?

....

14. Name two forms of carbon.

....

....

15. Why do all the elements in Group VII have similar chemical properties?

....

....

16. What are the three products made by the electrolysis of concentrated sodium chloride solution?

....

....

17. What happens to the reactivity of Group I metals as you go down the group?

....

....

....

18. Complete the table below:

	number of protons	number of electrons	number of neutrons	electron structure
$^{12}_{6}C$				
$^{14}_{6}C$				

19. Sodium chloride is an ionic compound.
   Draw a 'dot and cross' diagram to show how sodium chloride is formed from its elements.

20. a) Magnesium has an electronic structure of 2, 8, 2. To which group does it belong?

....

b) Magnesium can form ionic compounds. What charge do magnesium ions carry in such compounds?

....

How did you do?

1–5	correct ....start again
6–10	correct ....getting there
11–15	correct ....good work
16–20	correct ....excellent

COMMON TESTS AND SAFETY HAZARDS

COMMON TESTS

UNSATURATED HYDROCARBONS (ALKENES)

Bromine water is used to test for unsaturated hydrocarbons.
The orange-brown bromine water becomes colourless as it reacts with the unsaturated hydrocarbon.

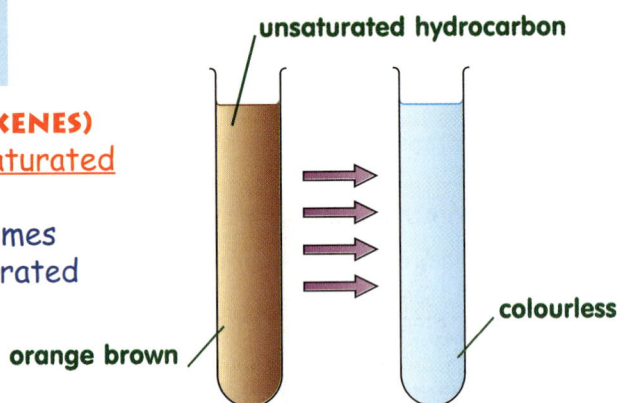

unsaturated hydrocarbon

colourless

orange brown

bromine water

CARBON DIOXIDE

The gas is bubbled through limewater.
Carbon dioxide turns limewater milky.

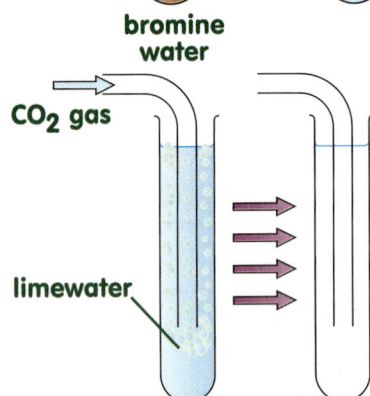

CO_2 gas

limewater

HYDROGEN

If a lighted splint is nearby hydrogen will burn with a 'squeaky pop'.

'squeaky pop'

H_2 gas

damp litmus paper

CHLORINE

Chlorine bleaches damp litmus paper.

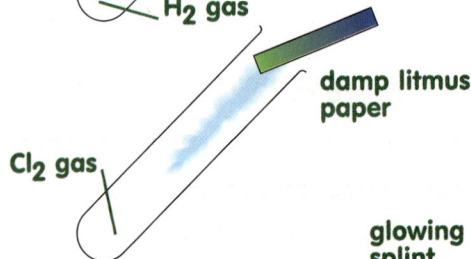

Cl_2 gas

glowing splint

OXYGEN

Oxygen relights a glowing splint.

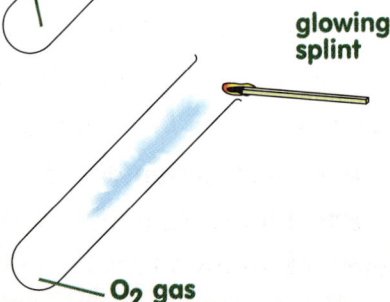

O_2 gas

SAFETY HAZARDS

OXIDISING
• Provides <u>oxygen</u> which allows <u>other</u> <u>materials</u> to burn <u>more</u> <u>fiercely</u>.

HARMFUL
• Similar to <u>toxic</u> but less dangerous.

HIGHLY FLAMMABLE
• Catches fire easily.

CORROSIVE
• Attacks and destroys <u>living</u> <u>tissues</u>, including <u>eyes</u> and <u>skin</u>.

TOXIC
• Can cause <u>death</u>, if <u>swallowed</u>, <u>breathed</u> in or <u>absorbed</u> through the skin.

IRRITANT
• Not corrosive but can cause reddening or blistering of the skin.

QUICK TEST

1. Sketch the hazard symbol for oxidising.
2. Sketch the hazard symbol for highly flammable.
3. Sketch the hazard symbol for toxic.
4. Sketch the hazard symbol for corrosive.
5. Sketch the hazard symbol for irritant.
6. What is the test for an unsaturated hydrocarbon?
7. What is the test for carbon dioxide?
8. What is the test for hydrogen?
9. What is the test for chlorine?
10. What is the test for oxygen?

Examiner's Top Tip
None of this is hard, it is just a case of learning all the points.

1. See above
2. See above
3. See above
4. See above
5. See above
6. Bromine water turns brown to colourless.
7. Gas is bubbled through limewater which turns milky.
8. Lighted split gives 'squeaky pop'.
9. Damp litmus paper bleached
10. Glowing splint relights.

TEMPERATURE

If the temperature is increased particles move quicker.
Increasing the temperature increases the rate *of* reaction *because the particles collide more often and with more energy so there are more successful collisions and the rate increases.*
a low temperature *slows reaction rate down*

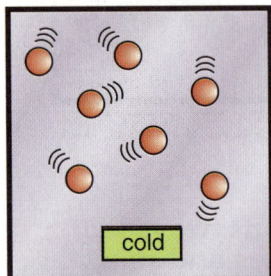

cold

a high temperature *speeds reaction rate up*

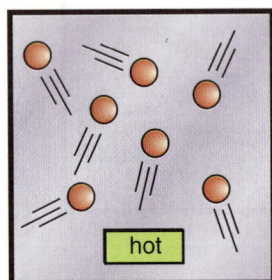

hot

INCREASING THE SURFACE AREA

The greater the surface area **the more chance of collisions occurring so the faster the rate of reaction.**

small surface area (larger pieces)

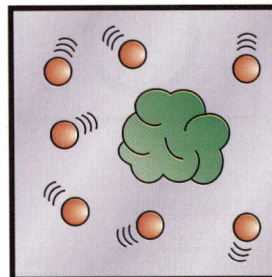

large surface area (smaller pieces)

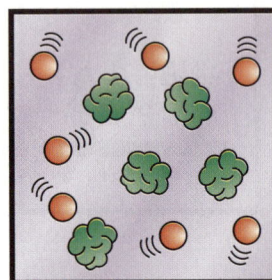

ADDING A CATALYST

- A catalyst increases the rate of reaction, but is not itself used up in the reaction.
- Catalysts are specific to certain reactions.

Examiner's Top Tip
When analysing graphs the reaction is over when the graph levels out.

ANALYSING RATES OF REACTION

The rate of a chemical reaction can be measured by:
- how fast the products are being made
- how fast the reactants are being used up.
The graph shows the amount of product made in three experiments.
The graph is steepest at the start of the reaction for all three experiments; it then starts to level out as the reactant particles get used up.
When the graph becomes level, the reaction has finished. The graph shows that Experiment 2 is faster than Experiment 1.
Experiments 1 and 2 make the same amount of the product so they both had the same amounts of reactants at the start of the reaction.
In Experiment 3 only half as much product was made.
This could have been due to Reaction 2 having a higher temperature, a greater concentration of reactant particles (or pressure for gases), a greater surface area or a catalyst being added to it.
This shows that the amount of the reactants was less at the start of Reaction 3.

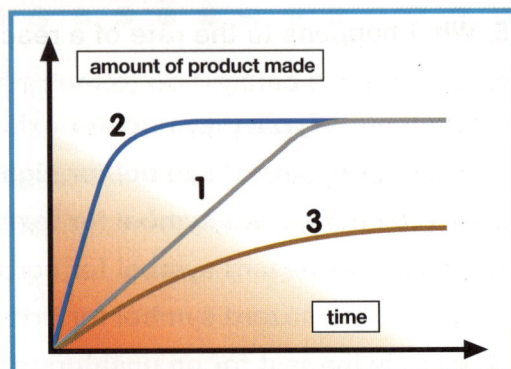

amount of product made

2   1   3   time

INCREASING THE CONCENTRATION OF DISSOLVED REACTANTS

The greater the concentration the more reactant particles there are in the solution. There will be more collisions and so the reaction rate is increased. For gases, increasing the pressure has the same effect as increasing the concentration of dissolved particles.

low concentration of particles

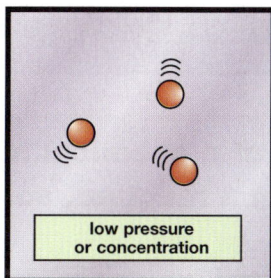

low pressure or concentration

high concentration of particles

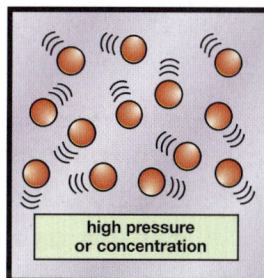

high pressure or concentration

RATES OF REACTION

Rates of reaction can be slow or fast:
- rusting
- explosions

Reaction energy

A chemical reaction can only occur if the reacting particles collide with enough energy (activation energy) to react. If they collide and do not have enough energy they bounce apart and do not react.

QUICK TEST

1. What happens if two particles collide but they do not have enough activation energy?

2. What happens to the rate of a reaction if the temperature is decreased?

3. What happens to the rate of a reaction if the concentration of the dissolved reactants is increased?

4. What happens to the rate of a reaction if the pressure of gas reactants is increased?

5. What happens to the rate of a reaction if the surface area of a reactant is increased?

6. What does a catalyst do to the rate of reaction?

7. Why can catalysts be reused?

8. How can the rate of a chemical reaction be measured?

9. Give four ways in which you could increase the rate of a chemical reaction.

10. Give three ways in which you could decrease the rate of a chemical reaction.

10. Decrease temperature; decrease concentration (pressure); decrease surface area
9. Increase temperature; increase concentration (pressure); increase surface area; add a catalyst
8. How fast reactant used up/product is made
7. Not used up during the reaction
6. Increases
5. Increases
4. Increases
3. Increases
2. Decreases
1. Do not react (bounce apart)

Examiner's Top Tip
Remember: small pieces have a larger surface area.

CATALYSTS AND ENZYMES

Catalysts:

- **can increase the rate of a chemical reaction**
- **are not used up during a reaction, so they can be used again**
- **are important in industry, as speeding up reactions reduces costs.**

Examiner's Top Tip
Catalysts are specific to a particular reaction, so only name a catalyst if you are sure that it works for that reaction.

HOW THEY WORK

You may have seen manganese (IV) oxide acting as a catalyst in the decomposition of hydrogen peroxide to produce oxygen and water. Catalysts work by providing an alternative pathway for a reaction to occur with a lower activation energy.

- The uncatalysed reaction pathway has a higher activation energy.
- The catalysed reaction pathway has a lower activation energy. More particles have enough energy to react and the reaction proceeds more quickly.

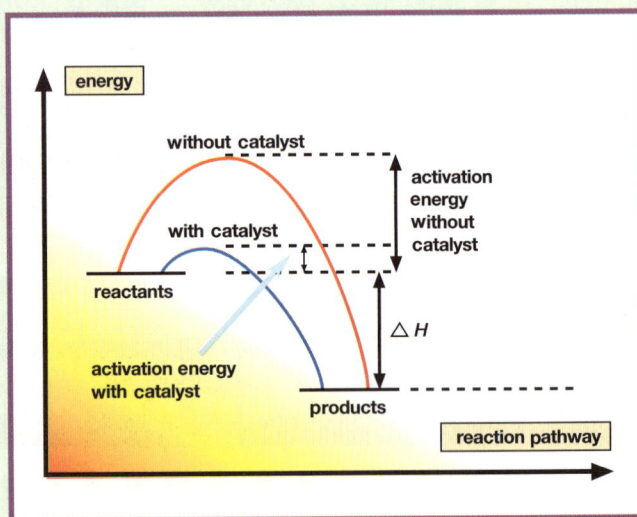

Diagram labels: energy; without catalyst; with catalyst; activation energy without catalyst; reactants; activation energy with catalyst; $\triangle H$; products; reaction pathway

ENZYMES

Enzymes are biological catalysts; they are protein molecules. Enzymes work well in warm conditions. If the temperature is too low the enzymes stop working as quickly.

Freezing food reduces the enzymes' activity, so the food remains fresh for longer. However, the enzymes will not have been destroyed, and on warming the food will continue to deteriorate. If the temperature is too high the enzyme will be denatured (damaged).

Enzymes usually stop working at temperatures above about 45ºC. Different enzymes work best at different pHs.

too hot

best

too cold

USES OF CATALYSTS

Catalysts and enzymes are used in many everyday situations:

BREAD-MAKING (FERMENTATION)

- In **fermentation**, yeast converts **sugar** into **carbon dioxide**, **ethanol** and **energy**.
- During bread-making yeast produces **bubbles** of carbon dioxide which gives the bread its **light texture**.

$$glucose \xrightarrow{yeast} carbon\ dioxide + an\ alcohol + energy$$

BREWING (FERMENTATION)

- Wine and beer are also made by **fermentation**.
- **Glucose** (sugar) from **fruit**, **vegetables** and **cereals** is converted into **alcohol** and **carbon dioxide**.

YOGHURT MAKING

- In yoghurt making **bacteria** are added to milk.
- These bacteria convert **lactose**, the sugar in milk, into **lactic acid**.

BIOLOGICAL DETERGENTS

- Biological detergents contain **protein-digesting** and **fat-digesting** enzymes (**proteases** and **lipases**) so they can get clothes cleaner.

INDUSTRIAL USES

- Enzymes that break down proteins (**proteases**) are used in the production of some baby foods.
- Enzymes that break down **starch** into sugar (**carbohydrases**) are used in soft-centred chocolates.
- **Isomerase** converts glucose into **fructose**. Fructose is much sweeter and so can be used in smaller quantities in slimming foods.

QUICK TEST

1. Why can catalysts be used again?
2. Why are catalysts used in industry?
3. A catalyst provides a reaction pathway with a lower activation energy. Why does this increase the rate of a reaction?
4. What are enzymes?
5. What happens to enzymes in cold conditions?
6. What happens to enzymes in hot conditions?
7. Why does bread have a light texture?
8. In brewing what ingredients can provide the glucose (sugar) for fermentation to occur?
9. Which enzymes break down proteins?
10. Which enzymes break down fats?

Examiner's Top Tip
Learn the different industrial uses of enzymes.

1. They are not used up 2. Speed up reactions; reduce costs 3. More particles have enough energy to react 4. Biological catalysts 5. They stop working as quickly. 6. They are denatured 7. Due to bubbles of carbon dioxide being produced during fermentation 8. Fruit/vegetables/cereals 9. Proteases 10. Lipases

EXOTHERMIC AND ENDOTHERMIC REACTIONS

- **Exothermic reactions give out energy.**
- **Endothermic reactions take in energy.**

ENERGY LEVEL DIAGRAMS

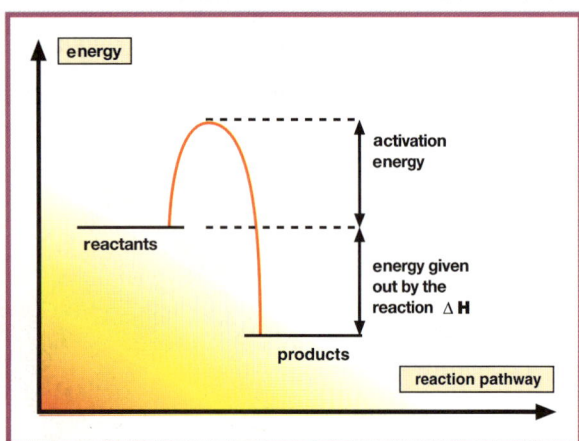

an exothermic reaction

- The products have <u>less</u> energy than the <u>reactants</u>.
- The <u>difference</u> in energy between the <u>products</u> and the <u>reactants</u> is the amount of energy given out by the reaction.
- The <u>initial</u> increase in the energy needed for reaction to occur (the activation energy) is required to break the bonds in the reactants and start off the reaction.
- Overall more energy is released through making new bonds than is taken in by breaking the old bonds.
- Catalysts provide an alternative reaction pathway with a <u>lower</u> activation energy.

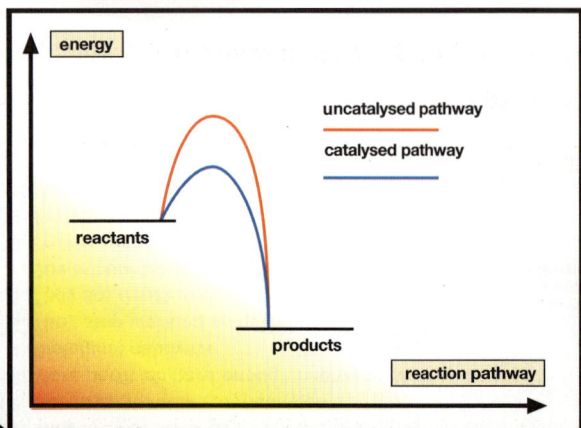

BOND ENERGY CALCULATIONS

Each chemical bond has a bond energy: this is the amount of energy that must be <u>taken in</u> to break one <u>mole</u> of bonds.

EXAMPLE
Formation of <u>hydrogen</u> <u>chloride</u>:

- $H_2 + Cl_2 \Rightarrow 2HCl$

Examiner's Top Tip
Breaking bonds requires energy to be supplied.

Bond energy in kJ per mole:
- **H – H   436**
- **Cl – Cl   242**
- **H – Cl   431**

Energy taken in to break bonds:
- **1 mole of H_2 = 436 kJ**
- **1 mole of Cl_2 = 242 kJ**
  Total = 678 kJ

Energy given out from forming bonds:
- **2 moles of HCl = (2 x 431)**
  Total = 862 kJ

The difference in energy between products and reactants:

Energy given out – energy taken in
= 862 – (436 + 242) kJ
= 862 – 678 kJ
<u>= 184 kJ mol^{-1}</u>

This reaction <u>gives</u> <u>out</u> more energy than it <u>takes</u> <u>in</u> so it is <u>exothermic</u>.
ΔH for the reaction = –184 kJ mol^{-1}

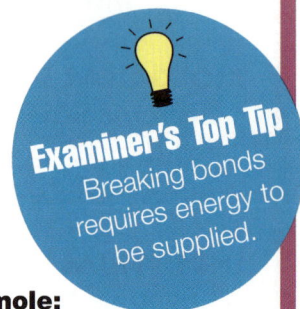

ENDOTHERMIC REACTIONS

In endothermic reactions energy, normally in the form of heat, is <u>taken in</u> from the surroundings. This is shown by a <u>decrease</u> in temperature. The thermal decomposition of calcium carbonate into <u>quicklime</u> (calcium oxide) and carbon dioxide is an endothermic reaction. A lot of heat must be taken in for the reaction to take place. The products have more energy than the reactants. The difference in energy between the products and the reactants is the <u>amount</u> of <u>energy</u> taken in by the reaction.

Overall more energy is taken in to break old bonds than is released by making new bonds.

energy level diagram: energy (y-axis), reaction pathway (x-axis); activation energy; products; reactants; energy given out by the reaction ΔH

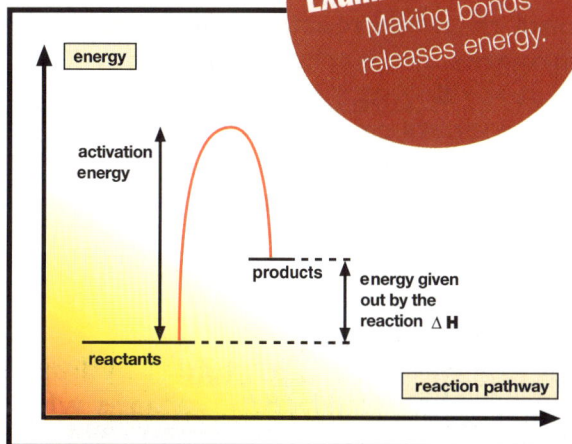

EXOTHERMIC REACTIONS

In exothermic reactions heat is <u>given out</u> to the surroundings. This normally causes a <u>rise</u> in temperature.
<u>Burning fuel</u> is an <u>exothermic reaction</u>, which gives out a lot of heat.

QUICK TEST

1. During a reaction the temperature increases. What sort of reaction has occurred?

2. How do you know burning coal is an exothermic reaction?

3. Sketch an energy level diagram for an exothermic reaction.

4. On the same diagram show the reaction pathway for the catalysed reaction.

5. On the diagram show the amount of energy given out by the reaction.

6. During a reaction the temperature decreases. What type of reaction has occurred?

7. Sketch an energy level diagram for an endothermic reaction.

8. When hydrochloric acid is neutralised by sodium hydroxide the temperature increases. Is this an exothermic or an endothermic reaction?

9. In a reaction, more energy is released through making new bonds than is taken in to break old bonds. What type of reaction has occurred?

10. In another reaction, more energy is taken in to break old bonds than is given out through making new bonds. What type of reaction has occurred?

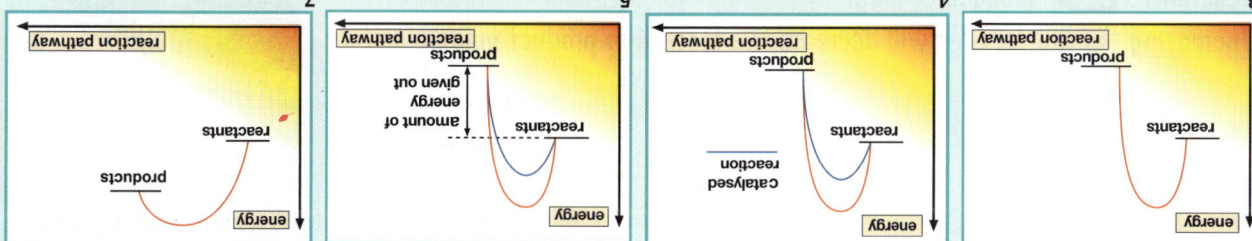

Answer diagrams 7, 5, 4, 3 (energy level diagrams showing reactants, products, reaction pathway, catalysed reaction, and amount of energy given out)

1. Exothermic 2. It gives out (heat) energy. 3. See below 4. See below 5. See below 6. Endothermic 7. See below 8. Exothermic 9. Exothermic 10. Endothermic

SIMPLE REVERSIBLE REACTIONS

Some chemical reactions are reversible; they can proceed in both directions (forwards and backwards).

- A + B ⇌ C + D

The products can react to form the original reactants.
If the forward reaction is exothermic (gives out heat) the backward reaction is endothermic (takes heat in).
The amount of heat given out and taken in must be the same.

EXAMPLE

The thermal decomposition of hydrated copper sulphate (hydrated means with water, anhydrous means without water)

water vapour

backward reaction

forward reaction

In the forward reaction heat is taken in (endothermic).
- hydrated copper sulphate ⇨ anhydrous copper sulphate + water
  (blue)   (white)

In the backward reaction heat is given out (exothermic).
- anhydrous copper sulphate + water ⇨ hydrated copper sulphate
  (white)   (blue)

DYNAMIC EQUILIBRIUM

If a reversible reaction takes place in a closed system (where nothing can escape) eventually an equilibrium will be reached.

It is a dynamic equilibrium: both the forward and backward reactions are taking place at exactly the same rate.

The conditions will affect the position of equilibrium (that is how much reactant and product are present at equilibrium).

reactants combine

product splits up

dynamic equilibrium

If the forward reaction is exothermic:
- reactants ⇨ products + heat
- Increasing the temperature will decrease the amount of product made.

If the reaction is endothermic:
- reactants + heat ⇨ products
- Increasing the temperature will increase the amount of product made.

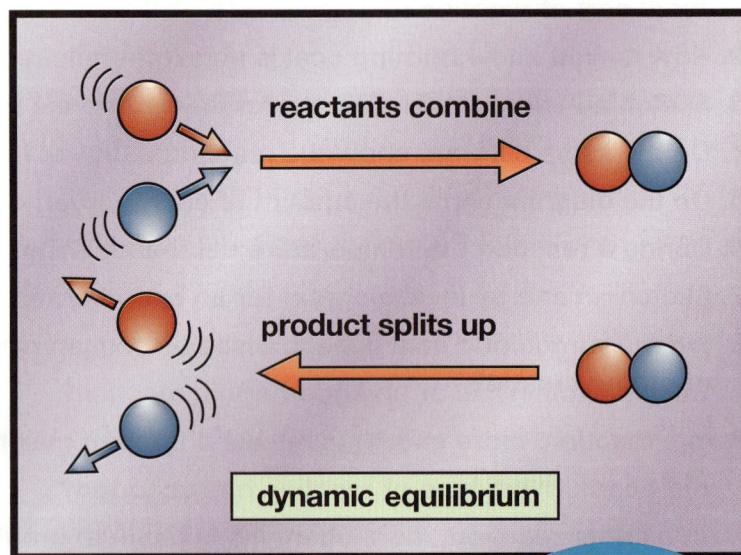

Examiner's Top Tip
In a dynamic equilibrium both the forward and backward reactions are still happening, but at the same rate so that they cancel each other out.

REACTIONS INVOLVING GASES

If the reaction includes gases count the number of gas particles on the left-hand side and the right-hand side of the equation.

reactants ⇨ products

fewer gas particles ⇨ more gas particles

• Increasing the pressure decreases the amount of product.

reactants ⇨ products

more gas particles ⇨ less gas particles

• Increasing the pressure increases the amount of product.

Examiner's Top Tip
Practise explaining how changes in temperature and pressure can change the amount of product made in a reaction.

REVERSIBLE REACTIONS

QUICK TEST

1. What is special about a reversible reaction?

2. If the forward reaction gives out energy, what type of reaction is it?

3. In the reverse reaction energy is taken in, what type of reaction is this?

4. What can be said about the amount of energy in each case?

5. Give the equation for a forward reaction that is endothermic.

6. Give the equation of a backward reaction that is exothermic.

7. In an exothermic reaction what is the effect of increasing the temperature on the amount of product made?

8. In an endothermic reaction what is the effect of increasing the temperature on the amount of product made?

9. This reversible reaction takes place in a closed system: $ICl(l) + Cl_2(g) \rightleftharpoons ICl_3(s)$
   What is the effect of increasing the pressure on the amount of product made?

10. This reversible reaction takes place in a closed system:

    $NH_4Cl(s) \longleftrightarrow NH_3(g) + HCl(g)$

    What is the effect of increasing the pressure on the amount of product made?

1. Can proceed in either direction
2. Exothermic
3. Endothermic
4. The same
5. Hydrated copper sulphate —> anhydrous copper sulphate + water
6. Anhydrous copper sulphate + water —> hydrated copper sulphate
7. Decreases amount of product
8. Increases amount of product
9. Increases amount of product
10. Decreases amount of product

THE HABER PROCESS

THE HABER PROCESS

This is an example of a reversible reaction.

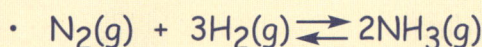

- $N_2(g) + 3H_2(g) \rightleftharpoons 2NH_3(g)$

Some of the nitrogen and hydrogen react to form ammonia. At the same time, some of the ammonia breaks down into nitrogen and hydrogen.

INDUSTRIAL CONDITIONS
- high pressure (200 atmospheres)
- quite high temperature (450°C)
- an iron catalyst.

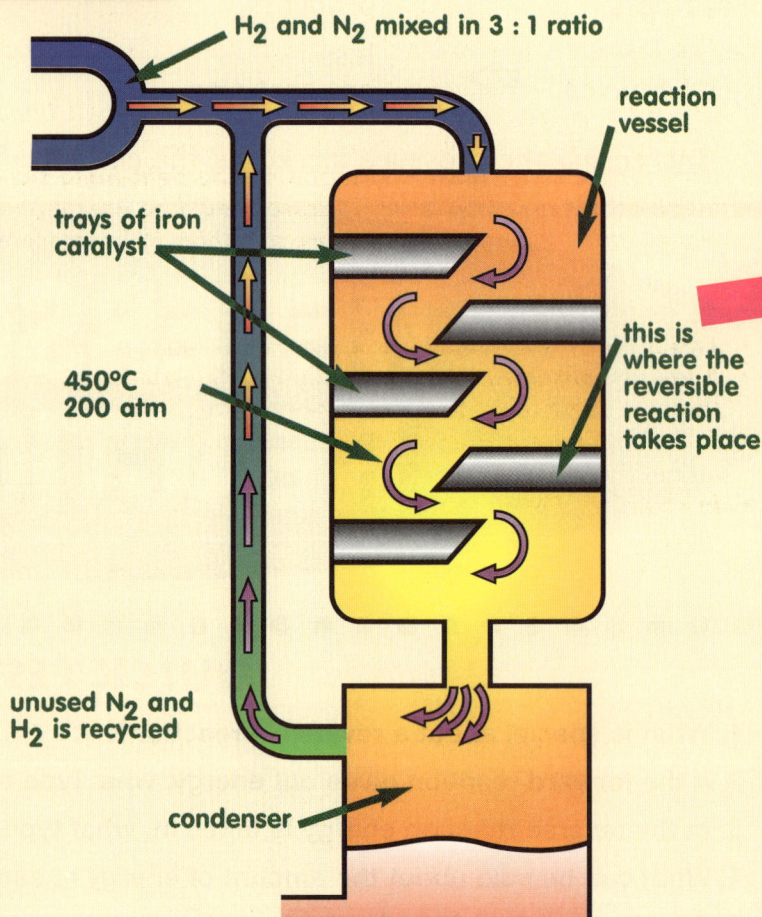

Examiner's Top Tip
Be able to explain the effect of changing both the pressure and the temperature in this reaction and why these compromise conditions are actually chosen.

H_2 and N_2 mixed in 3 : 1 ratio

reaction vessel

trays of iron catalyst

450°C 200 atm

this is where the reversible reaction takes place

unused N_2 and H_2 is recycled

condenser

USES OF AMMONIA

Ammonia can be oxidised to produce nitric acid.
Ammonia gas reacts with oxygen in the air over a hot platinum catalyst.

- $4NH_3(g) + 5O_2(g) \Rightarrow 4NO(g) + 6H_2O(g)$

The nitrogen oxide is cooled, and then reacted with water and more oxygen to form nitric acid.

- $4NO(g) + 3O_2(g) + 2H_2O(l) \Rightarrow 4HNO_3(g)$

The nitric acid can be neutralised with ammonia to make ammonium nitrate.
Ammonia can also be reacted with sulphuric acid to make ammonium sulphate.
These are both popular fertilisers.

- **Ammonia** is produced by the **Haber process**.
- **Ammonia** is made of **nitrogen** and **hydrogen**.
- The hydrogen is obtained from **natural gas** and the nitrogen is obtained from the **air**.

CHOOSING THE CONDITIONS

PRESSURE

- A *high* pressure is used because it *increases* the amount of ammonia made.
- There are *four* gas molecules on the left-hand side of the equation, *one* nitrogen and *three* hydrogen molecules.
- There are only *two* ammonia molecules on the right-hand side.
- *Increasing* the pressure encourages the forward reaction which increases the amount of ammonia because there are fewer molecules on the right-hand side of the equation.
- Ideally, the highest possible pressure should be used; however it is too expensive to build a plant which can withstand pressures greater than 200 atmospheres.

TEMPERATURE

- This is an *exothermic* reaction (gives out heat).
- A low temperature would actually *increase* the *amount* or *yield* of ammonia, but it would be at the cost of a much slower rate of reaction.
- A *higher* temperature would have a faster rate of reaction but, unfortunately, the amount of ammonia produced would be *lower*.
- In practice, a compromise temperature of 450°C is used. This gives a reasonable yield reasonably quickly.
- On cooling the ammonia *liquefies* and is removed.
- Any nitrogen or hydrogen that has not been converted into ammonia can be *recycled* to reduce costs.

CATALYST

An *iron catalyst* is used to *speed up* the rate of reaction and so *reduce* the cost of producing ammonia.

QUICK TEST

1. What does the Haber process produce?
2. From where is the hydrogen obtained?
3. From where is the nitrogen obtained?
4. Why is this described as a reversible reaction?
5. Why does increasing the pressure increase the yield of ammonia?
6. Why is a compromise pressure of 200 atmospheres used in practice?
7. What is the effect of decreasing the temperature on the yield of ammonia?
8. What is the effect of decreasing the temperature on the rate of reaction?
9. Why is a compromise temperature of 450°C used in practice?
10. What is ammonia used to produce?

Examiner's Top Tip
Remember the conditions used industrially.

1. Ammonia
2. Natural gas
3. Air
4. Nitrogen reacts with hydrogen to make ammonia; ammonia breaks up to form nitrogen and hydrogen.
5. 4 gas molecules on LHS; only 2 on RHS encourages the forward reaction
6. Too expensive at higher pressure
7. Increases yield
8. Slows reaction
9. Reasonable yield produced reasonably quickly
10. Fertilisers

RELATIVE FORMULA MASS

RELATIVE ATOMIC MASS (RAM)

The relative atomic mass (RAM) is used to compare the masses of different atoms. The relative atomic mass of an element is the average mass of its isotopes compared with an an atom of $^{12}_{6}C$.

4
2 **He**   mass number
         atomic number
         (or proton number)

RAM of helium = 4

24
12 **Mg**

RAM of magnesium = 24

RELATIVE FORMULA MASS

The relative formula mass of any molecule is worked out by adding together the relative atomic masses of all the atoms in the molecule.
- For carbon dioxide, CO_2:

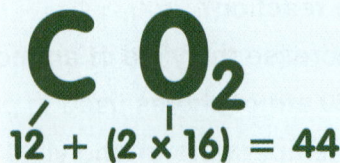

C O₂
$12 + (2 \times 16) = 44$

The relative formula mass of CO_2 is 44.
- For water, H_2O:

H₂ O
$(2 \times 1) + 16 = 18$

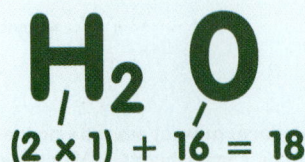

The relative formula mass of H_2O is 18.

FINDING THE EMPIRICAL FORMULA

- The empirical formula is the simplest ratio of atoms in a formula.

EXAMPLE
Find the empirical formula of magnesium oxide formed when 12 g of magnesium reacts with 8 g of oxygen atoms. Deal with the magnesium and the oxygen separately.

	Mg	O
state the number of grams that combine	12	8
change the grams to moles (divide by A_r)	12/24	8/16
this is the ratio in which the atoms combine	0.5	0.5
get the ratio into its simplest form.	1	1

- The simplest ratio of Mg : O is 1 : 1, so the formula is MgO.

CALCULATING THE PERCENTAGE COMPOSITION OF AN ELEMENT IN A COMPOUND

Percentage mass of an element in a compound $= \dfrac{\text{relative atomic mass} \times \text{no. of atoms}}{\text{relative formula mass}} \times 100\%$

EXAMPLE

Ammonium nitrate, NH_4NO_3, is used as a fertiliser.
Find the <u>percentage</u> <u>composition</u> of nitrogen in this compound.

- RAM of N = 14
- RAM of H = 1
- RAM of O = 16

The formula mass of NH_4NO_3 is:
- $14 + (4 \times 1) + 14 + (3 \times 16) = 80$

Percentage of nitrogen $= \dfrac{14 \times 2}{80} \times 100\% = 35\%$

- <u>Ammonium nitrate is 35% nitrogen</u>

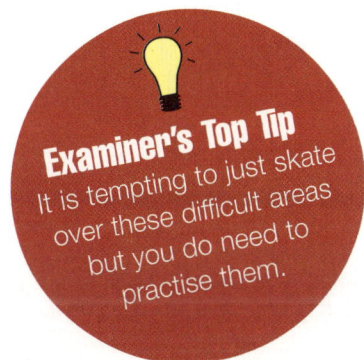

Examiner's Top Tip
It is tempting to just skate over these difficult areas but you do need to practise them.

QUICK TEST

1. Find the RAM of carbon, C.
2. Find the relative formula mass of nitrogen molecules, N_2.
3. Find the relative formula mass of oxygen molecules, O_2.
4. Calculate the relative formula mass of carbon monoxide, CO.
5. Calculate the relative formula mass of copper sulphate, $CuSO_4$.
6. Calculate the relative formula mass of calcium carbonate, $CaCO_3$.
7. Calculate the percentage of hydrogen in ammonium nitrate, NH_4NO_3.
8. Calculate the percentage of oxygen in ammonium nitrate, NH_4NO_3.
9. Find the empirical formula of sodium chloride formed when 7.1 g of chlorine reacts with 4.6 g of sodium:

   A_r of Na = 23, A_r of Cl = 35.5.
10. Find the empirical formula of iron oxide formed when 14.0 g of iron reacts with 6.0 g of oxygen:

   A_r of Fe = 56, A_r of O = 16.

10. Fe_2O_3
9. NaCl
8. 60%
7. 5%
6. 100
5. 159.5
4. 28
3. 32
2. 28
1. 12

BALANCING THE EQUATION

When hydrogen burns in oxygen, water is made.

- Hydrogen + oxygen ⇨ water

- H_2 + O_2 ⇨ H_2O

The formulae are correct, but the equation is not balanced because there are different numbers of atoms on each side of the equation. The formulae cannot be changed, but the numbers in front of the formulae can be changed.

HOW TO BALANCE AN EQUATION

Looking at the equation we can see that there are two oxygen atoms on the left-hand side but only one on the right-hand side.

So a 2 is placed in front of the H_2O:

- H_2 + O_2 ⇨ $2H_2O$

Now the oxygen atoms are balanced, but while there are two hydrogen atoms on the left-hand side there are four hydrogen atoms on the right-hand side.

So a 2 is placed in front of the H_2:

- $2H_2$ + O_2 ⇨ $2H_2O$

- *The equation is then balanced.*

Examiner's Top Tip
If you have to write the equation for a reaction write the equation in words first.

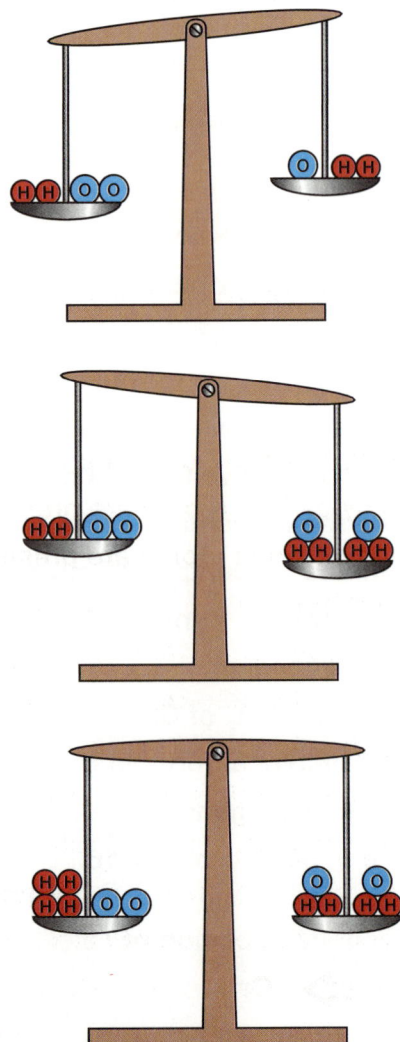

STATE SYMBOLS

State symbols can be added to an equation to show extra information. They show what state the reactants and products are in.
The symbols are:

- (s) for solid
- (l) for liquid
- (g) for gas
- (aq) for aqueous or dissolved in water

EXAMPLE

magnesium + oxygen ⟹ magnesium oxide

- $2Mg(s)$ + $O_2(g)$ ⟹ $2MgO(s)$

BALANCING EQUATIONS

- **Symbol equations show the number of atoms.**
- **There must be the same number of atoms on both sides of the equation: atoms cannot be created or destroyed.**

magnesium + oxygen ⟹ magnesium oxide

$2Mg$ + O_2 ⟹ $2MgO$

• • + ○○ ⟹ ●○ ●○

QUICK TEST

1. How many calcium atoms are present in $CaCO_3$?
2. How many carbon atoms are present in $CaCO_3$?
3. How many oxygen atoms are present in $CaCO_3$?
4. Why must there be the same number of atoms on both sides of the equation?
5. Balance the equation $Na(s)$ + $Cl_2(g)$ ⟹ $NaCl(s)$.
6. Balance the equation $H_2(g)$ + $Cl_2(g)$ ⟹ $HCl(g)$.
7. Balance the equation $C(s)$ + $CO_2(g)$ ⟹ $CO(g)$.
8. What does the state symbol (l) indicate?
9. What does the state symbol (aq) indicate?
10. Add the state symbols to this equation for the thermal decomposition of calcium carbonate:

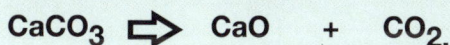

$CaCO_3$ ⟹ CaO + CO_2.

1. 1
2. 1
3. 3
4. Atoms cannot be created or destroyed.
5. $2Na(s)$ + $Cl_2(g)$ ⟹ $2NaCl(s)$
6. $H_2(g)$ + $Cl_2(g)$ ⟹ $2HCl(g)$
7. $C(s)$ + $CO_2(g)$ ⟹ $2CO(g)$
8. Liquid
9. Aqueous
10. $CaCO_3(s)$ ⟹ $CaO(s)$ + $CO_2(g)$

CALCULATING MASSES

CALCULATING THE MASS OF PRODUCTS

- The <u>equation</u> for a reaction can be used to <u>calculate</u> how much of a product is made.

EXAMPLE
What <u>mass</u> of water is produced when <u>8 g</u> of <u>hydrogen</u> is burnt in <u>oxygen</u>?
- RAM of H = 1
- RAM of O = 16

Write out the balanced equation:
- $2H_2(g) + O_2(g) \Rightarrow 2H_2O(g)$

Work out the relative formula mass:
- $2 \times (1 \times 2) + (16 \times 2) \Rightarrow 2 \times (18)$
- $4 + 32 \Rightarrow 36$

The formula mass is the relative formula mass in grams.

What does 1 g of hydrogen make?
- 1 g of hydrogen makes $\frac{36}{4}$ = 9 g of water

Multiply by the number of grams:
- 8 g of hydrogen makes 9 x 8 = 72 g of water

This calculation shows that if <u>8 g of hydrogen</u> is burnt in oxygen, <u>72</u> g of H_2O are made.

Examiner's Top Tip
Show all the stages in your calculations.

CALCULATING THE VOLUME OF GAS

One mole of a gas (the relative formula mass) will always take up a volume of 24 dm^3 or 24 000 cm^3.
This means that 28 g of N_2 will take up a volume of 24 dm^3, as will 71 g of Cl_2.
- RFM of N_2 = 28, RFM of Cl_2 = 71

$$\frac{\text{Volume of gas (dm}^3)}{24 \text{ (dm}^3)} = \frac{\text{mass of gas (g)}}{\text{RFM of gas}}$$

EXAMPLE
Find the volume taken up by 8 g of hydrogen, H_2.

$$\frac{\text{Volume of gas (dm}^3)}{24 \text{ (dm}^3)} = \frac{8 \text{ g}}{2 \text{ g}}$$

Volume of gas = $\frac{8}{2} \times 24$ dm^3
= 96 dm^3
- This calculation shows that 8 g of hydrogen will take up a volume of 96 dm^3.

CALCULATING THE MASS OF REACTANTS

- The equation for a reaction can also be used to calculate how much reactant should be used.

EXAMPLE

What <u>mass</u> of magnesium should be used to produce <u>60 g</u> of magnesium oxide?

- RAM of Mg = 24
- RAM of O = 16

Write out the balanced equation:

- $2Mg(s)$ + $O_2(g)$ ⟹ $2MgO(s)$

Work out the formula masses and the reacting quantities:

- 2 x 24 + 2 x 16 ⟹ 2MgO
  48 + 32 ⟹ 80

80 g of MgO is made from 48 g of Mg.

How much is needed to make 1 g of MgO?

- 1 g of MgO is made from $\frac{48}{80}$ g of Mg.

Multiply by the number of grams:

60 g of MgO is made from $\frac{48}{80}$ x 60 g = 36 g

This calculation shows that to produce 60 g of MgO <u>36 g</u> of Mg should be used.

QUICK TEST

1. Write out the word equation for the reaction between magnesium and oxygen.
2. Show this reaction as a balanced symbol equation.
3. Work out the relative formula mass of all the reactants and products.
4. If 48 g of magnesium is burnt what mass of MgO is produced?
5. What mass of magnesium should be burnt to make 30 g of magnesium oxide?
6. What volume is taken up by 10 g of Ne?
7. What volume is taken up by 8 g of He?
8. What volume is taken up by 28 g of N_2?
9. What volume is taken up by 56 g of N_2?
10. What volume is taken up by 7 g of N_2?

Answers (inverted):
1. Magnesium + oxygen ⟹ magnesium oxide
2. $2Mg(s) + O_2(g)$ ⟹ $2MgO(s)$
3. Mg = 24, O_2 = 32, MgO = 40
4. 80 g
5. 18 g
6. 12 dm³
7. 48 dm³
8. 24 dm³
9. 48 dm³
10. 6 dm³

CALCULATIONS INVOLVING ELECTROLYSIS

During the electrolysis of molten sodium chloride solution:
at the positive electrode chloride ions lose electrons to form chlorine molecules

- $2Cl^- \Rightarrow Cl_2 + 2e^-$

at the negative electrode sodium ions gain electrons to form sodium atoms

- $2Na^+ + 2e^- \Rightarrow 2Na$

These two half-equations are <u>balanced</u> because they both have the <u>same</u> <u>number</u> of electrons.
Half-equations can be used to <u>calculate</u> how much of a product has been made.

EXAMPLE
In the electrolysis of molten sodium chloride, <u>sodium metal</u> and <u>chlorine gas</u> are produced.
If 1.5 g of sodium is deposited at the negative electrode, what volume of chlorine is released at the positive electrode?
Write down the 2 half-equations:

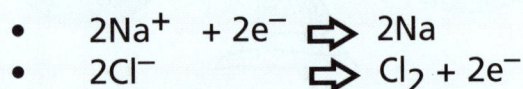

- $2Na^+ + 2e^- \Rightarrow 2Na$
- $2Cl^- \Rightarrow Cl_2 + 2e^-$

Write down the mass of 2Na and Cl_2

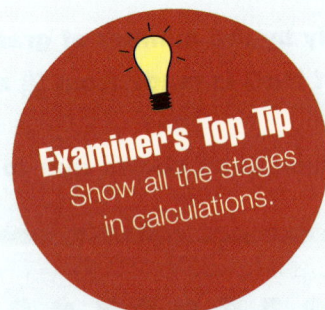

- 2Na Cl_2
- 2 x 23   35.5 x 2
- = 46g   = 71g

Examiner's Top Tip
Show all the stages in calculations.

As 1g of sodium is deposited, $\frac{71}{46}$ = 1.54 g of chlorine would be deposited.

As 1.5 g of sodium is deposited, $\frac{71}{46}$ x 1.5 = 2.32g of chlorine would be deposited.

This calculations shows that as <u>1.5 g</u> of sodium was deposited, <u>2.32 g</u> of chlorine gas, Cl_2, was released.
We can now work out the volume that <u>2.32 g</u> of chlorine would take up.

$$volume = \frac{mass}{formula\ mass} \times 24\ dm^3$$

$$volume = \frac{2.32}{71} \times 24\ dm^3$$

volume = 0.784 dm^3
The <u>2.32 g</u> of chlorine produced takes up a volume of <u>0.784 dm^3</u>.

OXIDATION AND REDUCTION

During **electrolysis** at the **negative** electrode **positively** charged ions gain electrons. This is **reduction**.

At the **positive** electrode **negatively** charged ions lose electrons. This is **oxidation**.

As both **reduction** and **oxidation** are occurring, this is a **REDOX** reaction.

Examiner's Top Tip
It is tempting just to read these sections, but you must practise them thoroughly.

ELECTROLYSIS

QUICK TEST

1. What happens during a reduction reaction?

2. What happens during an oxidation reaction?

3. What is a REDOX reaction?

4. During the electrolysis of Al_2O_3, Al^{3+} ions gain electrons. What type of reaction is this?

5. During the same process O^{2-} ions lose electrons. What type of reaction is this?

6. During the electrolysis of molten lead bromide, lead ions gain electrons. What type of reaction is this?

7. During the same process bromide ions lose electrons. What type of reaction is this?

8. During the electrolysis of aluminium oxide

   $$4Al^{3+} \quad + \quad 12e^- \quad \Rightarrow \quad 4Al$$

   Balance the second half-equation

   $$\underline{\quad}O^{2-} \quad \Rightarrow \quad \underline{\quad}O^2 + \underline{\quad}e^-$$

9. During the electrolysis of molten sodium chloride, 2.3 g of sodium is deposited. What mass of chlorine was produced?

10. During the electrolysis of molten sodium chloride, 2.0 g of chlorine gas is produced. What mass of sodium was deposited?

1. Gain of electrons
2. Loss of electrons
3. When reduction and oxidation occur
4. Reduction
5. Oxidation
6. Reduction
7. Oxidation
8. $6O^{2-} \Rightarrow 3O_2 + 12e^-$
9. 3.55 g
10. 1.30 g

THERMAL DECOMPOSITION

In **thermal** **decomposition** reactions a **substance** is broken down into **simpler** **substances** by heating.

EXAMPLE
The thermal decomposition of **limestone**:

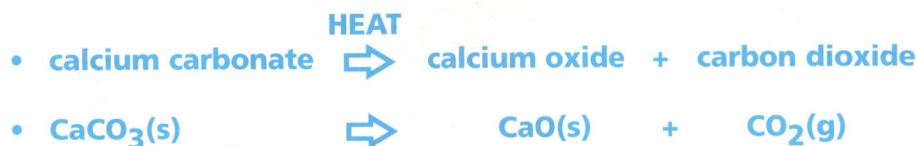

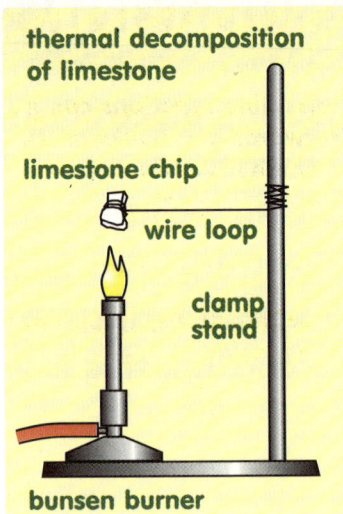

- calcium carbonate   **HEAT** →   calcium oxide   +   carbon dioxide

- $CaCO_3(s)$ → $CaO(s)$ + $CO_2(g)$

thermal decomposition of limestone

limestone chip

wire loop

clamp stand

bunsen burner

TYPES OF REACTION

NEUTRALISATION

In a **neutralisation** **reaction** an **acid** reacts with an **alkali** to form a **salt** and **water**.
- acid   +   alkali   →   salt + water

H^+ ions react with OH^- ions to form water.
- $H^+(aq)$ + $OH^-(aq)$ → $H_2O(l)$

EXAMPLE
The neutralisation of **sodium** **hydroxide** with **ethanoic** **acid**:
- sodium hydroxide + ethanoic acid → sodium ethanoate + water
- $NaOH(aq)$ + $CH_3COOH(aq)$ → $NaCH_3COO(aq)$ + $H_2O(l)$

bee stings are acidic and can be treated with sodium bicarbonate

OXIDATION

Many oxidation reactions involve the addition of oxygen.

EXAMPLE
The combustion of hydrogen:
- hydrogen + oxygen → water
- $2H_2(g)$ + $O_2(g)$ → $2H_2O(l)$

Oxidation also occurs during the electrolysis of aluminium oxide.

At the positive electrode:
- $2O^{2-}$ → O_2 + 4 electrons

Oxidation is loss of electrons.

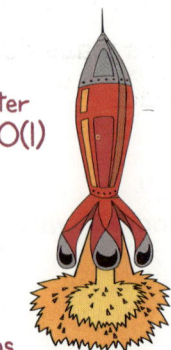

hydrogen can be used as rocket fuel

REDUCTION

Reduction is the opposite of oxidation. Many reduction reactions involve the loss of oxygen. Metals are extracted from their oxides by reduction.

EXAMPLE
Iron oxide is reduced to iron in the blast furnace:
- iron + carbon → iron + carbon dioxide
  oxide   monoxide

- $Fe_2O_3(s)$ + $3CO(g)$ → $2Fe(l)$ + $3CO_2(g)$

Reduction also occurs during the electrolysis of aluminium oxide:
- Al^{3+} + 3 electrons → Al

Reduction is the gain of electrons.

iron is used to make cars and trains

REVERSIBLE REACTIONS

Reversible reactions can go in <u>both</u> directions (forwards and backwards).
In these reactions the products can <u>react</u> to produce the original reactants.

EXAMPLE

- ammonium chloride $\rightleftharpoons$ ammonia + hydrogen chloride

- $NH_4Cl(s)$ $\rightleftharpoons$ $NH_3(g)$ + $HCl(g)$

cold water

solid ammonium chloride

ammonia and hydrogen chloride gases

gentle heat

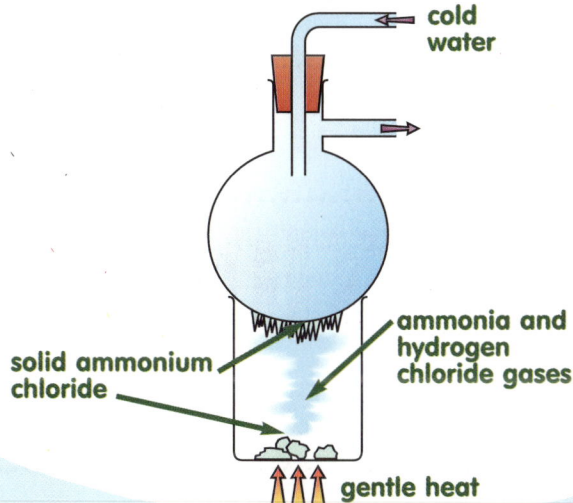

EXOTHERMIC REACTIONS

Exothermic reactions <u>give out</u> energy, normally in the form of <u>heat</u>: They get <u>hotter</u>.

Examiner's Top Tip
Be familiar with all these different types of reaction.

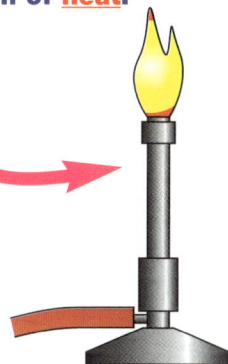

EXAMPLE

The burning of fuels, such as methane, gives out a lot of <u>heat</u> energy:

- methane + oxygen $\Rightarrow$ carbon dioxide + water
- $CH_4(g)$ + $2O_2(g)$ $\Rightarrow$ $CO_2(g)$ + $2H_2O(l)$

Examiner's Top Tip
The combustion of hydrogen is an oxidation reaction; it is also an exothermic reaction; a reaction can be of more than one type.

ENDOTHERMIC REACTIONS

Endothermic reactions <u>take in</u> heat energy, normally in the form of <u>heat</u>. They get <u>cold</u>.

QUICK TEST

1. What happens during a thermal decomposition reaction?

2. What is produced when calcium carbonate is heated?

3. What happens during a neutralisation reaction?

4. Write the word equation for the neutralisation reaction between sodium hydroxide and ethanolc acld?

5. Most oxidation reactions involve the addition of which element?

6. Give an example of an oxidation reaction that takes place during electrolysis.

7. What type of reaction produces iron from iron oxide?

8. What is special about a reversible reaction?

9. Why is the burning of fuel an exothermic reaction?

10. What is special about endothermic reactions?

10. Takes in energy (heat); gets colder
9 Gives out energy (heat); gets hotter
8. Can go in both directions
7. Reduction
6. $2O^{2-}$ —> O_2 + $4e^-$
5. Oxygen
4. Sodium hydroxide + ethanoic acid —> sodium ethanoate + water
3. Acid + alkali —> salt + water
2. Calcium oxide + carbon dioxide
1. Breakdown to simpler substances on heating

EXAM QUESTIONS – Use the questions to test your progress. Check your answers on page 95.

1. What is the chemical formula of ammonia?

....

2. Is the burning of fossil fuels an exothermic or an endothermic reaction?

....

3. Ammonium nitrate is a fertiliser. It is produced by a neutralisation reaction between ammonia and which other chemical?

....

4. Why is a catalyst used in a chemical reaction?

....

5. Name the enzyme which breaks down starch to sugar.

....

6. Name the enzyme which breaks down glucose to fructose.

....

7. Is this an endothermic or an exothermic reaction?

....

8. What is the name given to catalysts made by living things?

....

9. In a reaction magnesium is reacted with hydrochloric acid. What is the effect of increasing the surface area of the magnesium on the rate of the reaction?

....

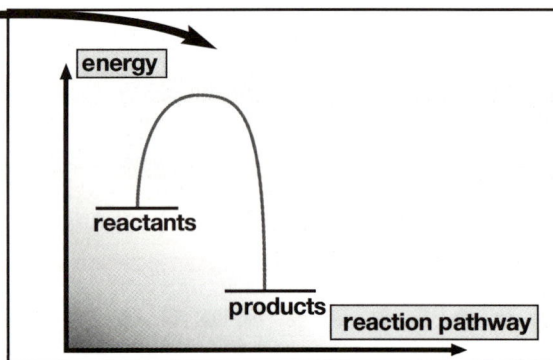

10. The diagram shows a chemical reaction energy profile. Which route shows the catalysed pathway?

....

11. At what temperature would an enzyme work best? Choose one answer:

    –10ºC   10ºC   40ºC   70ºC

....

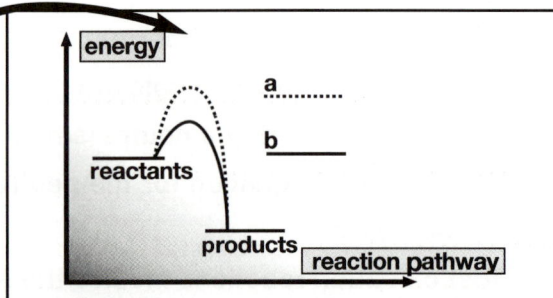

12. In an experiment calcium carbonate reacts with hydrochloric acid. The graph shows how much carbon dioxide is produced.

a) When is the reaction over?

....

b) Draw on the graph what you would expect to see if the acid was heated.

....

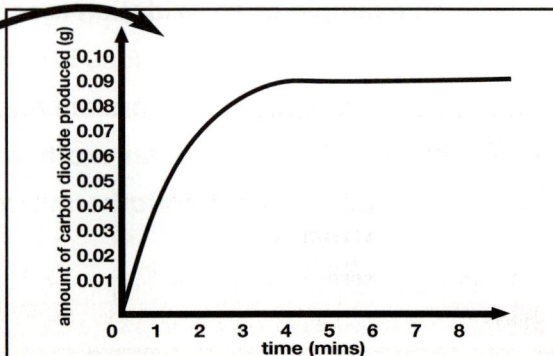

13. Write a balanced equation for the reaction between nitrogen and hydrogen to make ammonia.

....

14. What happens to an enzyme if it is heated above about 45°C?

....

....

15. Why does increasing the temperature of a reaction increase the rate of a reaction?

....

....

16. In the Haber process: $N_2(g) + 3H_2(g) \rightleftharpoons 2NH_3(g)$ (+ heat)
What is the effect of increasing the pressure on the yield of ammonia?

....

17. What is the effect of increasing the temperature on the yield of ammonia?

....

18. What is the effect of increasing the temperature on the rate of reaction?

....

19. What is the catalyst used in the Haber process?

....

20. Calculate the energy change for the reaction:
$H_2(g) + I_2(g) \Rightarrow 2HI(g)$
Bond energies (kJ mol^{-1})
H–H 436
I–I 151
H–I 299

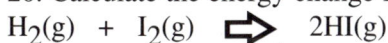

....

....

....

....

How did you do?

1–5	correct	....start again
6–10	correct	....getting there
11–15	correct	....good work
16–20	correct	....excellent

EXAM QUESTIONS – Use the questions to test your progress. Check your answers on page 95.

1. Name the type of reaction which takes place when iron is extracted from iron oxide.

....

2. Name the type of reaction in which sodium hydroxide reacts with hydrochloric acid to produce sodium chloride and water.

....

3. Complete the word equation:
calcium + oxygen $\Rightarrow$ ....

4. What is the relative atomic mass of lithium (Li)?

....

5. What is the relative atomic mass of calcium (Ca)?

....

6. Calculate the relative formula mass of methane (CH_4).

....

....

7. Calculate the relative formula mass of aluminium chloride ($AlCl_3$).

....

....

8. Calculate the relative formula mass of glucose ($C_6H_{12}O_6$).

....

....

9. Give the state symbols for the reaction:
$2Mg + O_2 \Rightarrow 2MgO$

....

....

10. Give the state symbols for the reaction:
$2H_2 + O_2 \Rightarrow 2H_2O$

....

11. Balance the equation $H_2 + I_2 \Rightarrow HI$

....

....

12. Balance the equation $Ca + HCl \Rightarrow CaCl_2 + H_2$

....

13. Balance the equation $C_2H_6 + O_2 \rightarrow CO_2 + H_2O$

....

....

14. During the burning of coal:

$C + O_2 \rightarrow CO_2$

If 12 g of carbon is burnt in plenty of oxygen, what mass of carbon dioxide is produced?

....

....

15. During the thermal decomposition of limestone:

$CaCO_3 \rightarrow CaO + CO_2$

If 50 g of calcium carbonate is heated, what mass of calcium oxide is produced?

....

....

16. During the neutralisation of hydrochloric acid with sodium hydroxide:

$HCl + NaOH \rightarrow NaCl + H_2O$

If 58.5 g of sodium chloride is produced, how much sodium hydroxide was used?

....

....

17. What volume is taken up by 32 g of oxygen (O_2)?

....

....

18. What volume is taken up by 19 g of fluorine (F_2)?

....

....

19. What volume is taken up by 5 g of neon (Ne)?

....

....

20. In the electrolysis of concentrated sodium chloride solution give the ionic half-equation for the reaction which occurs at the:

a) anode...

b) cathode...

How did you do?

1–5	correct	....start again
6–10	correct	....getting there
11–15	correct	....good work
16–20	correct	....excellent

Earth Materials

1. Igneous; sedimentary; metamorphic

2. Igneous

3. CFCs

4. Nitrogen

5. Sulphur dioxide

6. Oceanic

7. Metamorphic

8. a = crust; b = mantle; c = lithosphere; d = outer core;
   e = inner core

9. Calcium carbonate, $CaCO_3$

10. To make plastic bags and bottles

11. Plate tectonics

12. Convection currents caused by natural radioactive decay

13. Damage to buildings/trees/statues/plants
    and animals in lakes

14. a = youngest; d = oldest probably

15. Runny, easy to ignite; low boiling temperature

16. a) kerosene; b) petrol

17. Polymerisation

18. Ethane; propene

19. Alkanes show no reaction with bromine water; alkenes
    turn bromine water from orange-brown to colourless.

20. Jigsaw fit; similar rock sequences; same fossil record

Metals

1. Magnesium, zinc, iron, copper

2. Hydrochloric acid/sulphuric acid/nitric acid

3. Sodium hydroxide/potassium hydroxide/
   calcium hydroxide/ammonia solution

4. Universal indicator

5. Turns red

6. Less reactive

7. Red

8. Sodium, zinc, iron, gold

9. Iron is more reactive and displaces copper from the
   copper sulphate

10. Coke

11. Bauxite

12. Neutralisation

13. Electrolysis/reduction

14. So they can move

15. Carbon monoxide

16. a) Calcium chloride
    b) Potassium sulphate
    c) Sodium nitrate

17. $HNO_3(aq) + NaOH(aq) \Rightarrow NaNO_3(aq) + H_2O(l)$

18.

	solution		
metal	magnesium sulphate	copper sulphate	iron sulphate
magnesium	–	✓	✓
copper	X	–	X
iron	X	✓	–

19. Electrolysis

20. a) Alkaline
    b) Acidic

Structure and Bonding

1. a) Solid
   b) Gas
   c) Liquid

2. 1+

3. NaCl

4. Groups

5. Li/Na/K/Rb/Cs/Fr

6. F/Cl/Br/I/At

7. He/Ne/Ar/Kr/Xe/Rn

8. a) VI
   b) 16

9. No

10. Increasing atomic number

11. 2, 5; Group V

12. One outer electron

13. Bromine

14. Diamond and graphite

15. Same outer electron structure

16. Hydrogen, chlorine, sodium hydroxide

17. Increases

18.

	number of protons	number of electrons	number of neutrons	electron structure
$^{12}_{6}C$	6	6	6	2, 4
$^{14}_{6}C$	6	6	8	2, 4

19.

20. a) II
    b) 2+

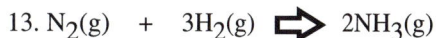

Chemical Change

1. NH_3

2. Exothermic

3. Nitric acid

4. It increases the rate of reaction (without being used up itself).

5. Carbohydrase

6. Isomerase

7. Exothermic

8. Enzymes

9. Increases the rate of reaction

10. b

11. 40°C

12. a) 4 min
    b) Line must be steeper, but not go higher than 0.09 g

13. $N_2(g) + 3H_2(g) \rightarrow 2NH_3(g)$

14. It is denatured.

15. The particles move faster; rate of collisions increases; more particles have enough energy to react; more successful collisions

16. It increases

17. It decreases

18. It increases

19. Iron

20. – 11 kJ mol^{-1} released so it is exothermic

Mixed

1. Reduction

2. Neutralisation

3. Calcium oxide

4. 7

5. 40

6. 16

7. 133.5 g

8. 180 g

9. $2Mg(s) + O_2(g) \rightarrow 2MgO(s)$

10. $2H_2(g) + O_2(g) \rightarrow 2H_2O(l)$

11. $H_2 + I_2 \rightarrow 2HI$

12. $Ca + 2HCl \rightarrow CaCl_2 + H_2$

13. $2C_2H_6 + 7O_2 \rightarrow 4CO_2 + 6H_2O$

14. 44 g

15. 28 g

16. 40 g

17. 24 dm^3

18. 12 dm^3

19. 6 dm^3

20. a) $2Cl^- \rightarrow Cl_2 + 2e^-$
    b) $2H^+ + 2e^- \rightarrow H_2$

INDEX